*New Voices Playwrights Theatre*

# Annual Anthology of Short Plays

# 2022

Edited by

## John Bolen

New Voices Playwrights Theatre
a 501(c)(3) corporation

P.O. Box 53921, Irvine, CA 92619-3921
newvoicesplaywrights.org
newvoicesplaywrights@gmail.com

# Table of Contents

# Foreword

In the writing of a play, after the character descriptions and not including the dialogue, the playwright gives two forms of instruction. One type is stage directions; the other type is parentheticals.

Stage directions are indented, in italics, and separate from the dialogue. These instructions describe entrances, exits, light and sound, set pieces, and most physical movement that the playwright feels is essential. The playwright explains which characters are on stage and any movement that is vital to the story, including such things as physical shtick or fight scenes. Stage directions inform the director and production artists collaborating in the staging of the play, who create the full world in which the play exists.

Parentheticals inform the actors and director. Written in parentheses and italicized, they explain how the playwright envisions the way a line may be delivered and to whom; how a theatrical pause or beat may show hesitancy or thought. Parentheticals describe how the dialogue is performed. In modern thought on the art of playwriting, parentheticals are to be used sparingly, allowing the actors to add their collaborative art to the process.

New Voices Playwrights Theatre creates full productions of the works of authors in our workshop. As a result, the playwrights are encouraged to be involved in the collaborative process, perhaps by helping with props, sets, costumes, moving set pieces, running tech, etc. Through this, they have the opportunity to fully comprehend how stage directions

and parentheticals serve to help design the world of a
play.

Watch for the **New Voices Holiday Plays 2022**, the
next in our series, available in October.

***John Bolen, Editor***
**Vice President**
**New Voices Playwrights Theatre**

# Abuela's Poem

By

Lillian Nader

Lillian Nader, M.Ed., is playwright, author, copyeditor, and retired educator. In 2019 and 2021, Lillian enjoyed seeing two of her holiday plays come to life on stage at Stage Door Repertory Theatre in Anaheim, CA. In addition to published plays in New Voices anthologies, she is the author of *Theep and Thorpe: Adventures in Space*, a science fiction novel for young readers. Her nonfiction publications include educational workbooks on cooperative learning in the classroom, and she is a contributing author to the e-book, *Muse & Ink: Soul Expressions Through Writing*.

Lillian enjoys writing books and plays for children and adults. She is an active member of New Voices Playwrights Theatre.

## CHARACTERS

Ana Louisa Hernandez, middle-aged Latina mom

Gabriel and Gabriela Hernandez, brother/sister fraternal twins, seniors in high school

Spirit of Abuela, appears behind a scrim dressed as La Catrina, a popular costume for The Day of the Dead holiday.

> *At rise Ana Louisa and the twins sit in their living room discussing plans for the holiday. It is October 31, Eve of The Day of the Dead (El Dia de los Muertos) celebration. In the living room is a special oblong table (altar) covered by a fine white tablecloth adorned with candles, photographs of deceased family members, incense, sweet foods, candy, and flowers.*

Gabriela: *(Whining.)* Mom, you said we could go to the Halloween party tonight.

Ana Louisa: Yes, of course, but you need to rehearse your part for the Dia de los Muertos celebration with our family this week, then you may go to be with your friends.

Gabriel: Mama, are you sure you don't want to recite Abuela's poem yourself instead of making us act it out? Abuela always read the poem to us on the Day of the Dead. Don't you remember?

Ana Louisa: Of course, I remember it very well. This is the first year your dear Abuela won't recite her poem for us.

> *Ana Louisa starts to cry.*

Gabriel: Please don't cry, Mama. Remember what they say: "Do not shed tears for they will make the path to your home slippery for those wishing to join you."

Gabriela: *(Shakes her head.)* What superstitious nonsense. Do people really believe that stuff?

Ana Louisa: *(To Gabriela.)* It isn't nonsense to celebrate traditions of honoring our loved ones who have passed on to the other side. It's necessary to show we're not afraid of death and recognize it as a part of the cycle of life. *(To Gabriel.)* I'm not crying, mi hijo. I've been cooking, and you know those onions make my eyes water. Now, as I was about to say, right before she died, your abuela made me promise that you would act out her poem for us to put on a show. You know how she loved to see you in plays.
Gabriela: *(Smiles.)* That's right! She always sat in the front row and gave us standing ovations at the end. Abuela didn't care if anyone else stood or not!

Gabriel: *(Laughs.)* And she let everyone know we were related.

Ana Louisa: She was so proud of you. You know, she left money in her will to make sure you both get a college education. That was very important to her. Now, let's get going with her poem.

*She hands each a copy of the poem.*

Gabriel: *(Reads the title.)* "Life and Death: a Dialogue".

Ana Louisa: I will read the introduction, then Gabriela will play the part of Life, and Gabriel, you will be Death.

Gabriel: No way! Why do I have to be Death? *(Clasps his chest and leans back dramatically.)* I'm too young to die!

Gabriela: Oh, give me a break; I'm just a few minutes older than you. I'm too young to die too. *(Stands with arms outstretched.)* I'm full of life.

Ana Louisa: Must you two argue about everything? Remember, we're trying to honor Abuela's wishes and her memory by reciting her poem.

> *Gabriel and Gabriela look at their mother and then at each other and shrug.*

Gabriela: We could flip a coin.

Gabriel: *(Takes a coin from his pocket.)* Okay. Heads, I'm Life; tails, you're Death.

Gabriela: Oh no you don't! It doesn't work that way. Heads, you're Life, and tails, you're Death. And we'll use my coin, not yours.

Gabriel: *(Tries to keep a straight face.)* Are you saying you don't trust me?

Gabriela: Humph, you've played that two-headed coin trick on me too many times, you coyote. *(She air-punches him.)* I definitely don't trust you. *(She takes a coin from her purse and flips it.)* I can't believe your luck, Gabriel. It's heads!

Ana Louisa: Well, that settles it. Now, let's talk about costumes. Gabriela, you can wear the skeleton costume for Death, and Gabriel can wear his regular clothes to represent Life.

Gabriela: Do I really have to wear that spooky skeleton costume? Abuela always dressed as La Catrina when she did the poem. She said La Catrina represented the fact that no matter how wealthy they became, rich folks died the same as everyone else. If I have to play the part of Death, I should at least get to wear Abuela's favorite costume. *(Facetiously.)* I sense that Abuela wants me to.

Ana Louisa: Oh, all right. You win. Now, hurry up and get changed into your costume. You'll find it hanging in the guest room closet. We'll make this a dress rehearsal to get you in the right mood.

*The house phone rings and Gabriel answers it.*

Gabriel: Hernandez residence. Gabe speaking... Oh, hi, Mrs. Thomas... yes, Mom is right here. *(Hands the phone to his mom.)* Carlotta's mom wants to speak to you. *(He shrugs.)*

Ana Louisa: Good afternoon, Mrs. Thomas... Yes, he's planning to attend the church Halloween party tonight. . . Oh, of course, I'll speak to him. He will do exactly as you request. No problem. *(She ends the call.).*

Gabriel: What was that all about?

Ana Louisa: She says Carlotta wants her permission to attend the Halloween party with you. Mrs. Thomas wants to make sure you'll bring her daughter home by 10:30 because tomorrow is a school day. I assured her you would. So, I need you to promise me you will honor her wishes and that you will be a perfect gentleman on your date tonight.

Gabriel: Are you sure she said 10:30? The party isn't over until 11:30.

Ana Louisa: Si, 10:30 or no date at all. And you must promise me. So, what do you say?

Gabriel: Yes, I promise.

Ana Louisa: You promise what? I need to hear you say it.

Gabriel: I promise I will be a perfect gentleman and have Carlotta home by 10:30 tonight. Actually, her parents are so strict, I'm surprised they're letting her go at all.

Ana Louisa: That's right. Count your blessings. Carlotta is a lovely girl, and I know you'll have a good time tonight even with the early curfew.

*Gabriel tries to sneak a piece of candy from the altar.*

Ana Louisa: Put that back on the table, Gabriel, and show some respect. I'm watching you! *(She shakes her finger at him.)*

*Gabriela enters, wearing an old fashioned, fancy evening dress. A black lace shawl is draped over her head and shoulders. She carries a bell.*

*(Starts to tear up again.)* You look so much like her; it takes my breath away.

Gabriel: Wow! You look amazing, mi hermana. Who would have guessed it?

*Gabriela smiles and curtseys.*

Ana Louisa: I will read the introduction, then Gabriel, you follow my cue:

"Life and Death: A Dialogue"
Feliz El Dia de los Muertos!
May the portals between Mortal Life and Death open wide

*Gabriela rings La Catrina's bell.*

So that our beloved spirits need not hide. *(Beat.)*
Now, to start the conversation,
Without equivocation,
Life speaks to Death and says...

*Gabriel is looking at his phone and misses his cue.*

Gabriela: *(Clears her throat.)* Gabe! That's your cue. You made such a fuss to play Life. It's your line, buddy.

Gabriel : *(Loudly overacting as Life.)*

Abuela's Poem

Death, Go away!
Come again when I'm old and gray.
Very, very old and gray.
Why do loved ones have to die?
Why do I?
Let's give Life Extension a try.

Gabriela: *(As Death, speaks to Life.)*

You are so quick to plead for life
Even one that's filled with strife.
All that you've been taught
About me... you've bought!
I've been given a bad rap,

And you've fallen for the trap.

Gabriel : *(As Life, motions to the children's portraits on the altar.)*

But why do innocents have to die,
Causing their families to cry?
Why must we endure such loss.
Who made you our boss?

Gabriela: *(As Death.)*

You take to grieving naturally,
Just like Jackie Kennedy.
Lift up the veil before your eyes;
Atone with me and realize
Your soul will rise to Immortality
Death is a part of life you see...
The just reward that's meant to be.

Gabriel: *(As Life.)*

How can Love let bad things happen
Such as the horror of the holocaust

And the plethora of disaster
Both before and after?

Gabriela: *(As Death.)*

God gave you mortals free will
A choice between good or evil.
To gently touch a life
Or add conflict and strife.
I am the solution not the problem,
The transition to a higher realm.
How you choose to live on Earth,
Will determine your rebirth.

> *A grey-haired lady appears behind a scrim dressed
> in the same La Catrina costume that Gabriela
> wears. She gazes at Ana Louisa, nods her head, and
> places her hand on her heart.*

Spirit of Abuela: Muchas gracias, mi corazon. Muchas gracias.

Ana Louisa: *(Makes the sign of the cross.)* De nada, mi Madre, con gusto.

> *Gabriel and Gabriela look at their mother, and then
> at each other and shrug.*

Gabriela: That went extremely well if I do say so myself. Are you satisfied with our performance, Mom?

Ana Louisa: Oh, yes. You both did me proud, and Abuela is very pleased; I'm sure of it. *(Beat.)* Now, you two go and change into your Halloween costumes while I make you something to eat before you go. You must be hungry, and they probably won't have anything but snacks at the party.

GABRIELA: What are you saying? I thought we decided I could wear the La Catrina dress tonight.

Ana Louisa: No, no, absolutely not! That dress is sacred and not to be worn to parties. You may only wear it at home for El Dia de los Muertos, November first and second. Only then for the reading of Abuela's poem. Is that understood?

Gabriela: Yes, Mother, I understand. The dress is sacred to you, and I would never forgive myself if I spilled something on it or did anything to harm it. I just really like the way I look in it and wanted to show it off at the party. I'm sorry. I'll find something else to wear.

*Gabriela exits.*

Gabriel: *(Checks his phone, grins.)* Yes! I have a date with Carlotta tonight. Her parents agreed to let me take her out after speaking with you on the phone. She just confirmed our date. *(He kisses Ana Louisa on the cheek.)* Thanks, Mamacita, you're the best. I know I wouldn't be taking Carlotta to the dance tonight if you hadn't vouched for me. I really appreciate it.

*Gabriela enters, wearing a skeleton costume and a mask designed for the occasion.*

Gabriela: *(With arms outstretched.)* Ta Da! I am Death, and I am not afraid!

Ana Louisa: Come into the kitchen you two; I've made a big batch of tamales in memory of Tio Juan, God bless his soul. *(Crosses herself.)* You know my homemade tamales were his favorite. And I made flan.

*Mother and son high five each other.*

Gabriela: *(Sarcastically.)* It's too bad Uncle Juan won't be here to enjoy it.

Ana Louisa: For shame on you, Gabriela! His spirit is here with us, and one day, God willing, you will know this is true.

Gabriel: She's right, Gabriela, you only pay attention to what's popular and what people think of you.

Gabriela: Not true! I think for myself and believe what I can see with my eyes. Do you see Tio Juan anywhere?

Gabriel: No, but I can smell his tamales, and they smell delicioso!

Ana Louisa:  Oh, and I thought you were educated and studied the words of Shakespeare. Gabriel, you played the part of Hamlet this year. What was that famous line you spoke to Horatio?

Gabriel: In Act 1, Scene 5, Hamlet says, "There are more things in heaven and earth, Horatio, than are dreamt of in your philosophy."

Ana Louisa: *(To Gabriela.)* Were you paying attention, mi hija? Why did he say this to his friend?

Gabriela: Oh, Mom. It's just a play. It's fiction. Make believe, not real life.

Ana Louisa: Answer the question, please. What happens in the play of Mr. Shakespeare that he spends time portraying?

Gabriela: Hamlet sees his father's ghost, but I don't see Uncle Juan's ghost, do you?

Gabriel: *(Grinning.)* I don't see his ghost, but I can almost taste his tamales. Let's eat. I'm starving!

*A loud car horn is heard outside.*

Ana Louisa: What is this noise I hear?

Gabriela: *(Heads toward the door.)* Oh, it's my date for the party. He's early.

*Ana Louisa blocks her path.*

Ana Louisa: No, no, no, my daughter. You know better than to think you're going out with a heathen who honks the car horn for you. Tell him to come inside and introduce himself, or you're not going anywhere with him. I'm sure your brother would be happy to give you a ride.

> *Gabriel groans.*

Gabriela: Oh, Mom! You are so old school.

Ana Louisa: *(Points to herself.)* Si, old school, that's me and your father too. He'll be home soon, and you know what he will say.

> *We hear the car horn again; the sound is longer and louder.*

Ana Louisa: You'd better text that boy...

> *Eerie music plays in the background. Gabriela tries to push past her mother. The Spirit of Abuela's black shawl drifts across the room and lands on Gabriela's head. Gabriela shudders from a sudden chill and looks at her mother in shock.*

Ana Louisa: You see, Gabriela? Abuela agrees with me. Now, you stay put until that boy comes to the door like a gentleman.


***End of play.***

# Assumptions

By

Lynne Bolen

Lynne Bolen, playwright, actor, producer, and director, has served on the Executive Board of New Voices Playwrights Theatre for over two decades. Her play, *Assumptions*, is included in Best American Short Plays 2011-2012, *Boulevard of Broken Dreams* in Best American Short Plays 2013-2014, *Baggage Game* in Best 5-Minute Plays, all published by Applause Theatre & Cinema Books. Her plays published in the New Voices Annual Anthology include *Spanish Masters* (2014), *Winners* (2015), *True Confessions* (2016), *A Fair to Remember* (2017), *Samantha Heart, P.I.* (2018), *Chicken Game* (2019), *Backs* (2020), *Small Change* (2021); and in the New Voices Holiday Plays, *Christmastime Machine* (2017) *Past, Future & Christmas Present* (2018), *On Target* [musical] (2019), and *Sunday News* (2020). Lynne's plays have been produced at Askew Theatre Company, Ashland, OR; Lion's Paw Theatre, St. Louis, MO; Niagara Univ, NY; Acadia Univ, Nova Scotia; Univ of Maryland; Univ of Rhode Island; Arizona State Univ; Univ of Northwestern, MN; Bethel College, KS; DePaul College Prep, IL; Hotchkiss School, CT; Oak Park High, CA; Drama West Productions; Stage Door Repertory Theatre; OC Pavilion Performing Arts Center; Chance Theater; Vanguard Theatre; Gallery Theatre; Empire Theatre; STAGEStheatre; Cabrillo Playhouse; Mysterium Theater; MUZEO.

## CHARACTERS

Grace, 20s-40s, female, non-Asian

Andre, 20s-40s, male, non-Black

Jordan, 20s-60s, any gender

> *It is present day and there is a table and two chairs. Andre is sitting at the table reading a document in a file folder. Grace, dressed in a tight jacket, skirt and high heels, opens the door and enters.*

Grace: Hello.

Andre: *(Quickly closing the folder.)* Hi.

Grace: *(Offers her hand.)* I'm Grace Lee.

Andre: *(Rises and shakes her hand.)* Grace, hello. Andre Washington.

Grace: A pleasure to meet you, Andre.

Andre: Likewise. Please, um, have a seat.

Grace: Thank you.

> *They both smile and sit awkwardly.*

Andre: So... Grace Lee.

Grace: I know. You were expecting me to be Asian.

Andre: What? No.

Grace: Really, it's okay. I'm used to it; it's happened my whole life.

Andre: I'm sorry. It's just that Miranda said you went to UCLA and are really smart...

Grace: ...and with that plus my last name Lee, you put two and two together.

Andre: It was a possibility. I apologize for assuming. Me of all people, right?

Grace: What do you mean?

Andre: You don't have to pretend.

Grace: I'm sorry, but I'm not following.

Andre: *(Teasingly.)* Didn't you assume I was black?

Grace: Why would I assume you were black?

Andre: Before we met. My name is Andre Washington. Admit it. You assumed I was black. Really, it's okay; I'm used to it. It's happened my whole life.

Grace: *(Smiling apologetically.)* Well, it was a possibility. Washington just seems like an African-American name.

Andre: Yeah, like George Washington.

Grace: Like <u>Den</u>zel *(Den'-zel.)* Washington.

Andre: It's Den<u>zel</u> *(Den-zel'.)*

Grace: Same thing.

Andre: Not to Den<u>zel</u>. You see his father's name was <u>Den</u>zel, and to differentiate, his name is pronounced Den<u>zel</u>.

Grace: Subtle difference. You're quite the expert.

Andre: Well, I like to keep track of all my Washington brothers.

Grace: Good for you, Andre. So, have you known Miranda long?

Andre: Yeah, we met at Berkeley. She is one classy lady.

Grace: Miranda has a great sense of humor. *(Provocatively.)* I assume she told you a bit about me?

Andre: Miranda speaks very highly of you. She thought we would get along well. What did she tell you about me?

Grace: She said you are very charming, and very wealthy.

Andre: Miranda is right.

Grace: What else did she say about me?

Andre: She said you wouldn't disappoint me.

Grace: Miranda is right. *(Beat.)* Did you make your money legally, Andre?

Andre: You cut right to the chase, Grace.

Grace: One of my strengths.

Andre: I started a tech company and Google bought it for a fortune; all perfectly legal.

Grace: I like a man who beats the odds.

Andre: *(Flirty.)* I think we are going to get along just fine.

Grace: *(Smiling seductively.)* So, Mr. Washington, shall we get down to business?

Andre: Let's do it. Ms. Lee, I would like to engage your services. Miranda said you're the best.

Grace: And the best is very expensive.

Andre: No worries, I can afford the best and will pay whatever high-price you normally charge your clients.

Grace: So you'll hire me at my usual rate?

Andre: Whatever it takes. You come highly recommended by Miranda.

> *Andre offers his hand and they shake. Grace stands and removes her jacket.*

Grace: Alright, let's get started.

Andre: I can't wait.

Grace: How do you plan to plea?

Andre: Not guilty, counselor.

Grace: I assumed so. But tell me, Andre, did you kill Vivienne Louise Anthony on the night of May 13?

Andre: No, I did not.

Grace: Your DNA was recovered from the crime scene.

Andre: That doesn't mean I killed her.

Grace: You were ID'd in the police line-up.

Andre: I'm innocent.

Grace: The evidence against you is overwhelming. The reason I agreed to take this case is because Miranda asked me to. Tell me what happened, and I can work a plea deal that'll keep you off death row.

Andre: I told you I'm innocent! Why the hell don't you believe me? Why does everyone assume I'm guilty?

Grace: Not assumptions, Andre, but implications based on the forensic evidence and witnesses.

Andre: People shouldn't jump to conclusions. Just because I'm rich, people are jealous and want to take me down. People are... The police are... The district attorney... Just because the district attorney is... Shit!

Grace: Dammit! Not again!

*Jordan emerges from the audience.*

Jordan: Cut!

Andre: Sorry, Jordan. Keep the camera rolling; I'll pick it up.

Grace: Focus, for God's sake!

Andre: Knock it off, you screwed up the last scene.

Grace: Only because you fed me the wrong lines.

Jordan: Hey, Kids, stop the constant bickering. Camera's rolling, lct's go. Okay, settle. Ready, and... action!

Andre: People shouldn't jump to conclusions. Just because I'm rich, people are jealous and want to take me down. Just because the district attorney assumes I killed Vivienne, doesn't mean I did. *(Earnestly pleading.)* Do you believe me, Grace?

Grace: Things are not always what they seem to be. I guess I shouldn't assume.

Andre: If you believe me, Grace, I know we can beat this case together.

Jordan: Cut! Okay, everyone, take five.

Grace: *(To Jordan.)* He keeps blowing his lines. I assume we'll be shooting this scene again after the break?

Jordan: You assume correctly. I need <u>more</u> from both of you. Hold tight, I'll be back in a minute.

 *Jordan exits.*

Grace: *(To Andre.)* You'd better get it right next time. And step it up! Jordan wants "more" from you.

Andre: Actually, Jordan wants "more" from <u>you</u>.

Grace: It's obvious Jordan meant you. You need to bring "more" when you say you're innocent, and then you need to explode when you say people jump to conclusions.

Andre: I have a director. Don't tell me how to act. Try working on your own acting. You're supposed to be sexy when you talk about getting down to business. Who'd want to hire a cold fish like you?

Grace: Cold fish! Really? You're crazy; Jordan loves what I'm doing. Jordan hasn't asked me to change anything. This is ridiculous. I can't work like this. Jordan! Jordan!!!

Andre: Stop being such a damned diva. It was embarrassing the way you went on about the lunch catering.

Grace: The food has been terrible on this shoot. In fact, everything has been terrible on this shoot. Especially you!

Andre: And you!

> *There is a pause.*

Grace: Please, can we just get through this awful scene without another take?

Andre: If you bring "more."

Grace: Truce. Seriously, I don't want to be here all night. I'm tired and I'm hungry. Craft services suck.

Andre: Truce.

> *They shake hands, firmly at first, but he holds on.*

*(Flirty.)* So... after we wrap tonight, how about the two of us going for a cold glass of beer and some grilled ahi tuna?

Grace: How about a cold glass of milk and some tuna casserole?

Andre: With crushed potato chips on top?

Grace; It's the twins' favorite! And frozen peas.

Andre: Ah, the glamorous movie-star life.

Grace: And after dinner, chapter three of <u>Captain Billy and the Gypsy Princess</u>.

Andre: *(Speaks with a pirate accent.)* Aye, and 'tis a saucy lass is the princess beauty. Arrr!

Grace: The twins love your pirate-speak. It's your best acting of the day.

Andre: It's my favorite role of the day.

> *They lovingly smile at one another. Jordan enters.*

Jordan: Okay, Kids, back to one. I assume you'll nail it this time.

> *Grace puts on her jacket and moves toward the door.*

Grace: You know what happens when you <u>assume</u>.

Jordan: Yeah, my actors get to wrap for the night.

> *Andre and Grace suddenly look at each other, earnestly. They give each other a high five.*

Andre & Grace: Let's do it!

Jordan: *(Sarcastically.)* <u>Assume</u> your positions. Back to one.

> *Grace exits.*

All right, everyone settle; quiet on the set; and action!

> *Grace enters.*

Grace: Hello.

> *Andre quickly closes the folder.*

Andre: Hi.

> *Grace offers her hand. Andre rises and shakes her hand.*

Grace: I'm Grace Lee.

Andre: Grace, hello. I'm Andre Washington.

> *Lights fade.*

### ***End of play.***

**Playwrights note:** How many times in a day do you assume that something will happen or someone will do something in the way you expect? When you watch a movie or a play, do you make assumptions that cause you to predict the ending, and aren't you pleased when you have guessed correctly? In writing <u>Assumptions</u>, my intent was for both the characters and the audience to make erroneous assumptions, so that their ideas twist and turn until they realize they should not assume anything. We all know what happens when you assume. In the 10-minute play, there are 18 assumptions!

# Back Over the Bridge

By

Pattric Walker

Pattric Walker is a musician, song writer, playwright, director, actor, and artist currently living and working in Southern California.   Of her plays that have been produced, she considers the world premiere of her full-length drama, *Dragons in New York* at the acclaimed Chance Theatre in Anaheim Hills her highest achievement so far.  In addition to plays, her book *33 Ways to Shape Up Your Slim Down*, various cartoons, poetry, and editorials have appeared in popular publications.

Pattric's plays have been published in previous editions of *New Voices Playwrights' Annual Anthology of Short Plays,* and *New Voices Holiday Plays*.

## CHARACTERS

Barbara, female, over 60, doesn't feel it, fit physically

May-Li, female, over 60, Asian, seriously works out

Tucker, male, over 60, a true Southern man, or proud Texan

August, male, over 60, quiet, sensitive

> *The living room in Tucker's condo in a senior community. Tucker, Barbara partners, May-Li, August partners, are playing bridge.*

May-Li:  One club.

Barbara:  One no trump.

August:  Pass.

Tucker:  Two no trump.

> *Barbara sets down her cards, and walks away.*

Barbara:  I can't do this anymore.

Tucker:  Do what?  We've got a solid two no trump that's goin' to give us this rubber.

Barbara:  It's boring.

Tucker:  Winnin' is never borin'.

August:  Is it the game?  We could change to poker, or gin.

Barbara:  It isn't the game.  I want to do something.

Tucker:  We are doin' somethin'.  We're playin' cards.

Barbara: Did you play cards when you were twenty?

Tucker: Damn right. Covered most of my college
tuition with gamblin'.

Barbara: That's admirable, Tucker, but it isn't the point.

May-Li:  I'm with Barbara.  Cards are getting to be old
hat.  What else can we do?

Barbara:  Thank you, May-Li.  The point is, Tucker, to
do.  I want to *do* something.  Be more active.

Tucker:  Like what?

Barbara:  Right now, I want to go bang some balls.

May-Li:  You didn't tell me.  Anybody I know?

August:  Oh, dear.

Tucker:  I hope you're not talkin' about mine.  I
answered the damn question.

Barbara:  I'm sorry, August.  I didn't mean to have such
an outburst.

> *Barbara collects her purse and gets her car
> keys.*

Tucker:  Hey, you're not leavin' are you?

Barbara:  Yes, I am.  I have to do something.

Tucker:  What about our two no trump?

Barbara:  You can finish it.  You were dummy, so move into my seat and play the rest of my hand.  I'm sure May-Li and August won't mind.

May-Li:  That would work.  *(To Tucker.)*  You'd rather not be dummy, right?

Tucker:  You'd better watch how you frame your questions, young lady.

August:  I doubt anything will change the outcome of this hand, unfortunately.

May-Li:  Are you sure you want to go home?  Isn't this better than being alone?

Barbara:  I'm not going home.

May-Li:  It's ten o'clock.  Where would you go at this hour?

Barbara:  I'm going to go shoot pool.

Tucker:  Yeah, right.  I hope that's supposed to be funny.

August:  No, she really does shoot pool.  I've see her in the billiards room at the senior center.  Today, even, right?

Tucker:  If you already played pool today, why do it again?  Sit down.  We're goin' to win this game.

Barbara:  I'm bored with cards, and I will not be put on a senior schedule.

August:  What's a senior schedule?

Barbara:  Having to do everything before four-thirty when the senior center closes.  We can't get a book, swim, or play shuffleboard under the lights when it's cool.  Apparently, the powers that be believe people over fifty-five are in bed by sunset.

August:  Well, we can't fight city hall.

May-Li:  You've got that right.  I got a notice saying I had to pay a fine, and penalties, because I failed to get a permit to hang paper lanterns around my patio.  Apparently, Chinese New Year is a special event.

Tucker:  That's un-American.

August:  Senior centers are city governed.  We have to be happy with what hours we have.

Barbara:  Why?  What about all the other hours?

Tucker:  Don't answer that.  It's probably another trick question.

August:  All I know is that I'd become a museum exhibit if the centers weren't open during the week days.  I can see the brass plate now:  "Mummy of old man discovered on sofa with Moby Dick".

Barbara:  That's the point, August.  If we let ourselves be old, we will be.  If we continue to do what we did when we were young, we'll stay young.  That's what I want.  Not to let myself get old.

May-Li:  We have to fight it.  I often can't sleep.  I was never like that before.  I sleep less, and if I can't at all, I get up and play computer games.

August:  Oh, my goodness.  You do?

Tucker:  What?

August:  I don't want to offend anyone.

Barbara: With us?  We've been playing cards for five years.  I don't think we truly could offend each other. Right, Tucker?

Tucker:  Ruffle a feather or two for a few minutes, but that's about it.

August:  All right, if you're sure.  I think computer games are way too violent.  I'm surprised to hear May-Li plays them.  Too much shooting in them.  I could be mistaken about that.

May-Li:  You're not.  A lot of them are vicious fighting.  I don't shoot people in the one I play.

August:  Oh, I'm glad.  I wouldn't like you as much if you shot people.

May-Li:  I use a bow and arrow or spear.  Does that help?

August:  I stand corrected.  I wish you hadn't said that.

Tucker:  Nothin' wrong with shootin'.

Barbara:  You think your twelve-point buck head would agree with that?

Tucker:  I wasn't talkin' about huntin'.

Barbara:  Surely you didn't mean people.

Tucker:  Don't you know me better than that, after all these years?  I'll let you apologize to me, and quit jumpin' to assumptions.  My daddy was a top shot. I've shot more bullets through the necks of bottles without even scratchin' the glass than I have deer.

Barbara: I'm sorry.  You still won't convince me you can take the South out of the man.

Tucker:  Not that I'd try.

May-Li:  I have an idea.  We could all play the computer game I play.  *(To Tucker.)* That is if you wouldn't mind us using your home theatre set up.  *(To everyone.)*  Here, it would make it feel as if you're really in the game.

Barbara:  How active is it?

May-Li:  It's intense.  Once your avatar enters the Amazon forests, you have to survive, and you're challenged by big cats, rabid monkeys, other players as hostile tribesmen...

Barbara:  You realize you're probably playing this game with six to sixteen year olds, right?

May-Li:  Just because I'm old doesn't mean I feel like it.

Barbara: Exactly.  But your video game has you sitting down, not doing.  Let's do something other than sit and, whatever.

May-Li:  You're right.  I'd do a lot more if we were allowed to.

Tucker:  Who's stoppin' you?

May-Li:  Society.  I love to walk and hike, but every club I called asked me my age right off.  I said I wanted to be in a general age group.  They don't have them.  We're being herded into like for like, and we don't have the option to join in to mix with all ages.  The same was true for an exercise class I wanted to take.

August:  That makes sense, though.  You wouldn't be able to keep up with a younger person's exercise routine.

May-Li:  Speak for yourself.  I use our gym every day.  I do overhand and curl pull ups, bench presses, bar weight squats, and lat lifts at one hundred and fifty pounds, according to the weights rack.

Barbara:  Rack; a word close to my heart.  I'm off.  Thanks for the start of a good game.

*Barbara starts to exit.*

May-Li:  Wait a minute.  You're still leaving?

Barbara:  There's a billiards room in Sunnymead.

May-Li:  What about your cataract?

Barbara:  I can see the balls clearly.  It doesn't get in the way at all.

May-Li:  I'm talking about the drive.  Sunnymead is thirty miles from here.

August:  She's right.  If your vision is blurry, you shouldn't be driving.

Barbara:  My vision is not blurry.  The cataract is worse in the left eye, which makes that eye blurry.  The right eye is good.  Oh, for Christ's sake, don't look at me like that.  I don't drive with a patch over the good eye.

Tucker:  What time would you be comin' back?

Barbara:  The place closes at one or two, I think.

Tucker:  Tell you what.  I'll ride shotgun and take you on for some games if you're up to it.  I can't drive at night any more, but I'll be able to tell you if you're going to hit somethin' or somethin's goin' to hit us.

August:  But if you can't see...?

Tucker:  I can.  Right before it happens.

*Everyone laughs.*

Barbara:  You're on!  It beats shooting racks by myself.  Let's all go.  We can play partners.

May-Li:  You bet.  I don't play, yet, but I'll give it a try.

August:  I should probably pass.

Tucker:  What the hell can you have goin' on that's so important you can't come out to play with us?

August:  Going to bed.  The chess club meets at eight tomorrow, then I go to senior stretching, nine pins takes me into lunch, which is about an hour in the cafeteria, then...

Tucker: That's it. I've had it. Of all the... You mean to tell me that, after all these years of bridge, we're no more to you than just another time slot in your routine?

Barbara: Tucker.

Tucker: No. I want to hear what the man has to say.

May-Li: One minute. August, it's good you keep busy. It's the why that worries me.

August: You just said why, keeping busy.

Barbara: Oh, August don't you see. You're on a senior schedule. Yes, you're keeping busy, but...

May-Li: Let me tell you what happened to me. One day, an older woman in the grocery line said to me, "our age". I looked at her. Her neck draped like the chiffon curtains over the bay window, and her face could pass for an aerial map of a river delta. I didn't realize I'd crossed over the bridge.

Tucker: What bridge? I thought you said you were in a market.

Barbara: Hush.

May-Li: I thought, I can't possibly look old like her. But it had happened. It was as if there was a bridge I didn't know was there. One day, it was a regular day. The next day, I was on the other side. The senior side.

Barbara: I stared at myself in the mirror the day it happened to me. We should name it the "our age" bridge.

August:  If I may express an observation.  Neither of you has wrinkles.  I mean, none that are significant, from a distance or numerous.  I believe some fine ones are unavoidable.

Barbara:  Thank you, August.

May-Li:  Yes, August, some are unavoidable.  What I didn't know was what else had changed.  People started to treat me differently; looked at me differently, if they noticed me at all.  I was phased out of my job.  Suddenly, I have all this time.  I tried to fill it with so-called senior activities, but I wasn't happy.  I didn't change, inside.  I still feel like a young person.

Barbara:  I firmly believe it.  If we think old, it will make us old.

May-Li:  We computer gamers chat.  The players range from six to a-hundred-and-six years old.

Barbara:  You're kidding, right?

May-Li:  He says he's a hundred and six.  I don't think it's some kid playing a prank.  He gets killed a lot because his avatar reacts so slowly.  I want to be like that man; still playing at something when I'm that old.

Tucker:  Maybe it's a woman thing.  Right August?

August:  I have to confess, I go through the motions, but I'm not happy either.  I feel as if I have to do something with the time; so much time.

May-Li: Too much time.  Then it hit me.  Bridges cross both ways.  I crossed back.  I can't be young again, but I can be who I am.  I can always feel young inside.  If that's doing young things, that's what I'll do.  I started lifting as a senior.  There's no such thing as too late to start.

Tucker:  And I'll bet you'd deck anyone who tells you that you can't.

May-Li:  With a right round kick.  I take Tae Kwon Do on Monday nights.  Mixed age group.

*A beat or two.*

August:  I hate it.

Barbara:  Now *you're* being rude.  May-Li was only trying to...

August:  The way I've been living.  Since I moved here, I've felt like I'm in some sort of military school.  Everything's regimented; and the rules, God, there are so many rules.  And it's not just the facility's rules.  The seniors make up more of their own rules.  Oh, and the busybodies.  Apparently they have nothing else to do but watch me.  I planted an azalea in my little front yard, and someone turned me in to the office.  It's not an approved flower.  Can you believe that?  I can't even plant a flower I like in my three-by-five front yard.

*Barbara comforts August; calms him.*

You're right.  I've been trying to just keep moving, zombie like.  I lost me.  And I almost lost all of you.  No, you're not just an activity. If we had to skip a week, I'd get anxious.  Our discussions and friendships have been a lifeline to me.

*Tucker extends his hand to August to shake, turns it into a man hug.*

Tucker:  Welcome back to the young side of the bridge.

Barbara:  Have you ever shot pool, August?

August:  No.  Only three cushion billiards.

Barbara:  Yes!  I've always wanted to learn that.

August:  Really?  They have a billiards table?

Barbara:  Yes, and I know where there are several other places that specialize in it.   Snooker, too.

Tucker:  Hold on there.  How about tonight, in deference to our beginner, we shoot eight ball.  *(To May-Li.)*  I'll be your partner.  Cards wasn't the only gamblin' I did to pay tuition.

May-Li:  I'm yours.

Barbara:  *(To August.)*  Remember, this is pool.  You *want* to drop a ball *into* a pocket.   Got it?

August:  Deal.

Barbara:  Promise you won't beat us all up with your stick?  I hear pool is a no brainer compared to billiards.

May-Li:  If he does, I can use mine as a spear and defend you.

August:  Oh, my.  I surely hope this is the right path.

Tucker:  C'mon, August, no feet draggin'.  We're goin' to bang some balls.

*All start to exit.*

### ***End of play.***

# Curveball

By

Linda Whitmore

***Curveball*** was first produced at Stage Door Repertory Theatre in Anaheim, Calif., in June, 2022, directed by Geoffrey Gread, and starred Jeremy Krasovic, Charlie Battaglia, and Autumn Browne.

Linda Whitmore is a playwright and screenwriter living in Southern California. She is a founding member of New Voices Playwrights Theatre & Workshop.

Her plays have been produced at STAGEStheatre, CA; Chance Theater, CA; Cabrillo Playhouse, CA; Costa Mesa Playhouse, CA; Vanguard Theatre, CA; Garden Grove Playhouse, CA; Gallery Theatre, CA; Empire Theatre, CA; Mysterium Theater, CA; and Stage Door Repertory Theatre, CA.

## CHARACTERS

John, male, 40s-50s,

Marla, female, 60s-70s

Nick, male, 40s-50s

> *At rise, a lectern faces the audience upstage in front of about a dozen folding chairs with their backs to the audience. To the right of the lectern is a bouquet of flowers and a large photographic portrait of Melissa on a tripod. John sits in the front row facing the lectern. In the back row, nearest the audience, Marla and Nick sit next to each other. Other actors can sit on chairs or there can be the assumption that the chairs are filled. John rises self-consciously and walks awkwardly to the lectern, unfolding a piece of paper he will read from.*

John:  Hi. Uh. Thank you all for coming today. I certainly wish I could see you under difference circumstances, but life has a way of throwing people a curveball. Such was Melissa's life. Anyway, as most of you know, I was kind of tasked... against my will... with saying a few words about Melissa today. This was her idea, and who am I to say no to her? She was the love of my life; or rather, became the love of my life. So this is one of the hardest things I've ever had to do. How do I capture in words Melissa's free spirit and joy of living? Her warmth and loyalty? Like most of us, she was a self-contained contradiction. She could be obstinate, but she was forgiving. We had a fight once and she locked me out of the house when I was naked. *(He laughs.)* That was the obstinate part. The fact she let me back in moments later... that was the forgiving part. I don't even remember what the fight was about. That was life with Melissa. She could be petty but she was open-minded and the best friend you could ever have. She could be spontaneous and funny. But she was the best listener I ever met. She was creative and insightful. And she was, of course, whip smart. When we met, I was writing for a small magazine and she was teaching at a private school in Long Beach. I think we would have ended up together... well, in a way, we did... but I think we probably would have gotten married if my career hadn't dragged me all over the country to Dallas, Portland, Minneapolis, Boston. There was always a next chapter for me. Maybe I thought, when I decided to hang up my reporter's notebook, Melissa would be there. With her kindness and empathy. Her laughter and her tears. Her humor and strength of character. Perhaps the most amazing thing about her is that she was such an amazing person; that she embraced life so tightly... despite the tragedies that befell her. As most of you know... perhaps some of you don't... is that Melissa had a tumultuous life To put it mildly. Her father died when she was young. She got married at a young age. Too young, she told me. And she had a daughter named Kaylee, who was the light of her life. That kid was Melissa's life.

> *In the back row, Nick leans over and whispers something to Marla. Nick starts to stand, but Marla prevents him.*

And as life does, it threw Melissa a curveball. Her first husband and their daughter died tragically in a car accident. When she told me over the phone, I could hear a hollowness in her voice that I never heard before.

I immediately offered to return to Southern California, but she insisted that she didn't want to be a bother. That was Melissa: Even as she lived through the worst thing that could happen to a person, she insisted she could weather it alone. She moved in with her mother. And she seemed to be doing well... for a while. But life had other plans. Her mother was diagnosed with cancer and, after a brief illness, died.

> *In the back row, Marla leans over and whispers to Nick. Marla starts to stand, but Nick prevents her.*

This would break most of us. And at this point, it did. It broke Melissa. This is the only time in the decades I knew her that her spirit seemed broken. I was listening to this happen long distance, and it broke me, too. She checked herself into… into and institution. She was only there briefly. I can't imagine what she was going through. You would think life couldn't throw anything else at Melissa, right? Well, like before, life proved it plays by its own rules. Not ours. Shortly after she was discharged, she felt a lump in her breast. She was diagnosed with Stage 4 breast cancer. When she told me that over the phone, I did something very uncharacteristic: I quit my job in Boston and moved in with her in Pasadena. Her last year was *(He tears up.)* difficult for her; and me. But especially her. I watched, in slow motion, as the… the spark dimmed in her eyes. The surgery scarred her body. The radiation sapped her strength and made her hair fall out. I drove her to the doctor's office and to her therapy. I did all the housework. I read to her. She never complained... even though she had to eat my cooking! All of these horrible things that happened to Melissa unfortunately made her into... I hate to speak ill of the dead, as they say... a world-class pessimist. She took every circumstance and spun it into a worst-case scenario. If we planned to go on a trip, she would say we might not be able to find hotel rooms, that the car would break down or, worse, that we'd get into an accident... and probably die. She could take a glass that was full and, by the time she was done, not only was the glass empty... there was no glass! Many of my friends, and even hers, called Melissa "an acquired taste." "Prickly." "Human Valium." And I get that. But the last year of her life, when I lived with and cared for her, I could see why every calamity that befell her had made her cynical and negative. For years, when I would phone my friends to tell them I was going to be in town, they were eager to see me. But they wouldn't want to meet up if Melissa was going to be there. You know who you are *(He laughs gently.)* But I don't blame you. She was the product of her experiences, many of them, as I have said, tragic. But I don't like to dwell on that. I focus on her humanity. Her humor. Her compassion. My love for her was unlike any love I've experienced with any other person. We accepted each other's differences. We respected each other. We were a team. In the end, my love was bittersweet. Perhaps I could have revolved my life around her more: put the brakes in my career. Stayed in Southern California. But then, if we had spent more time around each other, perhaps our love wouldn't have been so deep and abiding. And so, goodbye, Melissa. You touched so many lives. And you changed mine. I'll never forget you. I'll see you on the other side, my love.

*John slowly folds up the eulogy.*

Uh, there are some refreshments in the back of the room. We have the room for another 15 minutes.

*He steps away from the lectern and walks to the back of the room. There are soft drinks and cookies on a table. He grabs a bottle of water. Nick and Marla rise and slowly approach John.*

Nick: Hi, I'm Nick Weber. That was a lovely eulogy.

John: Hi, Nick. I'm John Corelli.

*Nick and John shake hands.*

Marla: I'm Marla Landon. Thanks for speaking.

*John and Marla shake hands.*

John: Melissa kinda made me promise to do it. Maybe she knew I'd go easy on her. How do you know her?

Nick: John, I'm… I'm Melissa's ex-husband.

John: I'm sorry? She never mentioned she had another husband.

Nick: She didn't, John. I was her only husband. And we had no children. Melissa never had a child. Not that I know of.

John: Uhhhhhh. I don't understand.

Nick: There was no child. And there was no car accident.

Marla: John, I'm Melissa's mother.

John: Now I'm really confused.

Marla: Melissa was ill, John. She was diagnosed with schizophrenia when she was in college. She graduated and got a job teaching.

Nick: That's where we met. We taught at the same school.

John: Why would she… why did she tell me that her husband and child had died in a car accident? And that her mother had died?

Marla: She was on medication for a while...

Nick: ...but she stopped taking it. I couldn't persuade her to keep taking it. Said it made her dull. But when she was off her meds, the voices in her head returned. It was heart-wrenching. It was like watching her descend down a … a long staircase into the dark. Once, after I got home from grocery shopping, I was in the driveway unloading bags; I turned around and she was standing there with a butcher knife! Scared the hell out of me! I said, "Honey, why do you have that knife?" And she said, "To keep people from stealing our food."

Marla: We'd talk on the phone and she was totally convinced that her co-workers were trying to kill her.

Nick: Her students, too! Fourth-graders!

Marla: She heard whispers. Like muffled conversations in her head, like if you walked into a dinner party of 30 people talking, but you couldn't discern any specific thing being said. It was awful, John.

Nick: She did tell you the truth about being institutionalized. She was, for a while.

Marla: Her father, who's still very much alive by the way, and I requested a psychiatric hold. We thought she was a danger to herself and others. But that was only for 72 hours. After that, she couldn't be held against her will.

Nick: I tried to stay with her, John. But I couldn't help her. She was the only person who could help herself.

Marla: After the divorce, she fell off her father's and my radar. In fact, my husband, Ted... he gave up on her. He refused to come today. He felt he had done everything he could do for her, but if she refused treatment and refused to speak to us, he was done with her. After she lost her job, we suspected she was homeless for a time.

John: Homeless! I... I would have known!

Marla: She was a very good liar, John. And from what you said, with you living all over the country, it would have been impossible for you to know.

Nick: After the divorce, I moved to San Diego and remarried. I have two kids now.

John: I'm… I'm stunned.

Marla: We almost interrupted your eulogy to correct you, but thought this might be a more… more diplomatic way to handle things.

Nick: I'm glad you were with her at the end. She deserved better than life gave her, that's for sure.

Marla: Yes, thanks so much for caring for my daughter. She… she certainly didn't ask to be sick. And that sickness consumed who she was.

John: I loved her, Mrs. Landon... If you don't mind my asking, how did you find out about her death?

Marla: I saw the obit in the paper. And I called Nick.

John: Ah, that makes sense.

Nick: Well, I better head back down. It was nice to meet you, John. And thanks again for helping Melissa at the end. I would have known she was sick…

*Nick trails off, nearly crying.*

Marla: There was no way for you to know, Nick.

*Nick and John Shake hands. Nick hugs Marla, then exits.*

Marla: Tell me, John, what is your most indelible memory of Melissa?

John: Wow. Good question… I guess it would have been when I was visiting L.A. once, years ago; from Portland, I think. She told me to meet her at the Griffith Observatory. I show up and she's carrying a… a basket. And I'm like, what's with the basket? It was a picnic lunch. Dinner, actually. Sandwiches, fruit, wine and chocolate. We sat on the grounds around the observatory and ate, drank and watched the sun set. It was so romantic. So spontaneous. One of those L.A. moments. I was so… happy that night; with her. Surrounded by all this… this natural beauty; I thought to myself, how lucky I am to be in that moment; with her; together… What about you?

Marla: Oh, lemme think… There were so many times. Maybe the best was when her father and I taught her how to ride a bike. Ted had taken off the training wheels and she was really scared. At first, she refused to pedal. But I told her, "If you don't pedal, the bike will fall over." She wanted to make sure we wouldn't let go. And we told her, of course now. We each ran along either side of the bike and after she built up a head of steam, we let her go. And of course...

John: ...She fell?

Marla: No, she rode like the wind! Fast, like an unbridled horse! I looked at Ted. And we smiled at each other. In that moment, it was like the three of us were one. We had created this... this perfect little human. She was such a delight as a child.

John: I wonder… I wonder if I should tell the rest of the people here the truth… They all signed the guestbook. I could reach out to each one...

Marla: ...What good would that do?

John: I'm a journalist, Mrs. Landon. My inclination is toward the truth.

Marla: Call me Marla, please. I understand, but why not just let her memory be, John? As you said, Melissa was an acquired taste, through no fault of her own. Let each of us live with our own memories of her.

John: I guess you're right. Thanks for coming, Marla. And thanks for telling me about Melissa.

Marla: You of all people deserved to know. Well, I should  be getting home, too. Will you need help going through her effects?

John: I hadn't thought of that. Probably because I thought she didn't have any living relatives. Yes, I guess. If you don't mind.

Marla: Call or email. My info is in the guestbook.

John: Thanks.

Marla: Of course, John. Goodbye.

John: Goodbye, Marla.

> *They hug and Marla exits. John looks out over the audience. He has a thousand-yard stare.*

John: Can we ever really know another person?

**_End of play._**

# Glimpse of Glory

By

Michael C. Buss

Michael Buss is a playwright/author now living in Santa Ana, Southern California.  He was the second President of New Voices Playwrights Workshop, of which he is a founding member.

Michael's short plays have nearly all been produced in Southern California: The Theatre District, CA; Chance Theater, CA; STAGEStheatre, CA; Vanguard Theatre, CA; Cabrillo Playhouse, CA; Costa Mesa Playhouse, CA; Stage Door Repertory Theatre, CA; The Gallery Theatre, CA; Empire Theater, CA; Newport Theatre Arts Center, CA. He has also had full length workshop productions at South Coast Repertory, STAGEStheatre, and Stage Door Repertory Theatre.

Most of Michael's Holiday Plays have been assembled and edited into an anthology entitled **Seasonings** (deliberate pun) which is available either directly from the playwright, or from Amazon.

NOTE: The playwright has extensively researched the Renaissance period of this play. Whereas the general scenario and characters are real, as are also the *white shirts,* the play remains a work of fiction.

## CHARACTERS

Girolamo Savonarola, male, 50s. Prior of San Marco, in Florence.

Niccolo Machiavelli, male, mid-30s. Diplomat, politician, philosopher.

Cardinal Cesare Borgia, male, late 20s. Bastard son of Pope Alexander VI, Rodrigo Borgia.

> *It is 1497 at the Priory of San Marco in the city of Florence, Italy. At rise we see Fra Savonarola kneeling in prayer at a wooden reading bench. His cane lies next to him. There is a short balustrade downstage, indicating the scene takes place on a balcony. Machiavelli stands in a spot to one side.*

Machiavelli:  From his early years as a mumbling ascetic, this man, Friar Girolamo Savonarola, has become the most significant influence on public affairs, religious, political, and  international, in the Italian state of Florence. His fiery preaching draws such crowds that during the season of Lent he is obliged to occupy the huge Cathedral of Santa Maria del Fiore, more commonly known as the Duomo, on account of its huge, unsupported dome engineered, as you may know, by Filippo Brunelleschi. Friends and enemies jostle in a temporary truce. After all, they are in church. We shall pay him a visit. It is the year of our Lord, 1497.

> *Spotlight fades rapidly as Machiavelli exits. There is a pause; then we hear banging on the door, offstage. Savonarola looks up and rises to his feet with the help of his cane.*

Savonarola:  *(Grumbling.)* I hear you! Patience, I pray you. Is there nowhere I can be left in silence with my God?

> *Enter Cardinal Borgia followed by Machiavelli, who both pause on seeing the friar.*

Cardinal:  Our apologies for having disturbed you in your religious duties.

Savonarola:  Ah... Cardinal Borgia! And you, my friend, Machiavelli. To what do I owe the somewhat dubious honor of your visit?

Machiavelli:  Dubious, good Friar? Dubious? I fear you may misjudge our intentions, which can be none other than to praise and encourage such a man through whom such peace has come to the people of Florence and kept us from the raging violence of the French King Charles.

Cardinal:  *(With total insincerity.)* Indeed. And our Holy Father in Rome, himself sends you his felicitations with the desire that you will ever be a faithful servant within our Holy Mother Church.

Savonarola:  These flattering words from the lips of such notable men make me wonder whether their softness should give rise to trepidation.

Cardinal:  Father Savonarola, it is true that the Pope views with concern the content of your fiery sermons; your condemnations of usury, and alleged corruption in the Holy See.

Machiavelli:  And you cannot be unaware that in spite of the widespread affection with which you are revered in Florence there are others...

Savonarola:  Ah, yes. The Oligarchs. The Arrabbiati. We have our differences.

Machiavelli:  Precisely. They are getting irritable.

Cardinal:  And that same irritation sometimes intrudes upon the Holy Father's mild disposition, such that we come to enquire of you the purpose of, how shall I put this? Of the...

Machiavelli: *(Hesitating.)* The white shirts!

Cardinal:  Exactly!

Savonarola:  *(Pausing.)* The white shirts?

Machiavelli:  Yes.

Cardinal:  The white shirts! These boys, mere teenagers, skipping around like little lambs with the words of our Lord Christ dripping from their lips. Such never has been seen before.

Machiavelli:  "Dripping" is a bit strong. But you know what we mean.

Savonarola:  Have you never read the words of the prophet Isaiah, "And a little child shall lead them?"

Cardinal:  What of it?

Machiavelli:  No, not I

Savonarola:  The prophet speaks of lions and lambs lying down together in peace. Both lions and lambs are to be found here in Florence.

Machiavelli:  Metaphorically speaking.

Savonarola:  Yes, metaphorically. And they are NOT at peace. For the rich oppress the poor, manipulating government to tax them, and to enlarge their coffers with the heavy burdens of usury. Meantime the poor resort to the rolling of dice, drinking, dancing, fencing, stealing and lying to eke out whatever livelihood they may. The lions kill the lambs. And with every sunrise the victims of the night are carted away for burial outside the city.

Cardinal:  And the children?

Savonarola:  You see, the word of God, which I expound, seems only to have temporary effects upon those who clamor about the pulpit. They are too addicted to their ways. But the children...

Cardinal:  ...Ah, yes, the children!

Savonarola:  The children are not yet inured in their parents' sins. They are yet malleable, amenable to the ways of the Lord.

Machiavelli:  Indeed, I have beheld them quietly sitting about the feet of Fra Domenico while he instructs them in the sayings of Jesus.

Savonarola:  Impressive?

Machiavelli:  It is a most unexpected sight.

Cardinal:  We also, in our holy mother church, take great care of children, bringing them into the faith ere they reach the age of ten.

Savonarola:  But here I note a difference. A profound difference.

Cardinal:  In what way?

Savonarola:  It's no secret that your priests, many of whom are known to frequent the local brothels, also lay claim to the flesh of pubescent boys, in the name of bringing grace and enlightenment to them.

Cardinal:  Friar, you must watch your words. They are dangerous calumnies. For you speak against those whose calling it is to lay hands on the sick and dying, ministering in the place of Christ to give life.

Savonarola:  *(His speech becoming that of a passionate preacher.)*  And so it should be! But when those hands which have caressed the secret parts of innocent children, then uphold the blessed sacrament, having us believe that God's grace flows through those same hands to transform bread into the body of Christ, those priests have violated their calling, they have become mere charades, with their pretense of holiness. They are bereft of God, dried husks fit only for the fire!

> *Fury has begun to build up inside the Cardinal. He reaches inside his robes for a dagger, moving aggressively towards Savonarola.*

Cardinal:  *(Hot with anger.)* Your tongue should be ripped from your foul mouth, you son of the devil.

*Machiavelli intervenes to prevent the attack.*

Machiavelli:  Cardinal Borgia! Desist, I beg you! It is not for you to dispense what you perceive as justice for the insults offered to the ministers of your church. Though I would offer that the matter of which he speaks is not exactly a secret amongst the faithful, and a matter of scorn in the drinking dens of Florence.

Cardinal:  *(Still riled up.)* Whose side are you on?

Machiavelli:  On nobody's side. I simply watch - observe. And as the truism goes, nobody's perfect!

Cardinal:  Maybe, but what about him? His meddling with children?

Savonarola:  *(Easing back.)* Your eminence, I admit I spoke with some heat but a few moments ago.

Cardinal:  You can say that again!

Savonarola:  Were it not for the passion stirred within me, I should have found less hostile words to put the case. But as to its essence, I can retract nothing.

Cardinal:  *(With some resentment.)* We understand you well, and regret that you have dared to shine such light upon such practices.

Machiavelli:  *(A touch of sarcasm.)* There, we are once again becoming more reasonable. I commend you both.

Cardinal:  Oh, don't be such a clever... what shall I say? A clever... mediator.

Machiavelli:  I try to see things all ways round.

Cardinal:  Then try to see this! He attacks me for abusing children...

Machiavelli:  Not the best way to put it, but...

Cardinal:  I agree. But what about these white shirts? After all, it was to make enquiry about these children that we came in the first place.

Machiavelli:  I had almost forgotten.

Savonarola:  All right. Let's get to it. What about the white shirts?

Machiavelli:  Tell us, then, how many young people, all boys I believe, do you have in your school? Should I even call it a school?

Savonarola:  That will do.

Cardinal:  So how many?

Savonarola:  At the last count - about three thousand.

Cardinal:  Holy Mother of God! A veritable army!

> *At this, Savonarola visibly winces. Machiavelli recoils in some surprise.*

Machiavelli:  Well, I knew it was a lot; they're running around everywhere. But... three thousand?

Cardinal:  This is incredible. What did you do with them?

Savonarola:  What do kids of that age normally do? They roam the streets, and probably get into trouble with shop-keepers, candle-makers, tanners, weavers, blacksmiths and the like. Anything to cause mayhem, have fun and get a few coins to spend.

Cardinal:  Exactly the same in Rome.

Savonarola:  But I give them lunch. Then they sit and listen. And I teach them about the life of Jesus, who was once a boy like them.

Machiavelli:  But not with all the japes these little knaves get up to.

Savonarola:  You could safely say that! But listen, these children know nothing of heaven and hell, or the love of God, until we teach them. They soon realize that the behavior they see in the adults about them probably dooms most of them to the fires of hell.

Cardinal:  Unless...

Savonarola:  Unless, they repent.

Machiavelli:  So they become little evangelists. I know. They've even been knocking at my door.

Cardinal:  Really?

Savonarola:  What did they say?

Machiavelli:  Well, the first ones were very nice. They asked if I ever went to hear the preaching of the famous friar?

> *Savonarola acknowledges this with a smile and slight bow. The Cardinal rolls his eyes.*

Machiavelli:  They seemed most anxious for my soul, and that I ought to cast my cares upon the Lord, that he might save me.

Cardinal:  But you're no better than an atheist! How did you take that?

Machiavelli:  I prefer to say I am not a believer in the doctrines of the church, if you'll excuse me, Cardinal, for one moment.

Savonarola:  But they came back?

Machiavelli:  Yes, they did; getting more insistent. They told me, somewhat rudely, I might add, that my material possessions mattered more to me than being in good keeping with the love of God. Let's face it; this was getting to be heavy stuff.

Savonarola:  No, no. They are right. This is what we've taught them.

Cardinal:  Taught them? They have no defense against what you teach them. They are mere children, unable to read or write.

Machiavelli:  In this I concur with the Cardinal. Dear friar, you have taken advantage of their innocent minds to fill them with your extremist religious babble.

Savonarola:  *(Indignantly.)* I have made them into young soldiers of the cross. They know the Gospel and they spread it to the whole City at this time of Carnival.

Machiavelli:  Yes, we know that Carnival time is famous for its debauchery, so I suppose a horde of child evangelists cannot be all bad.

Savonarola:  Indeed not.

Machiavelli:  But some of them are officious and rude, running into the gambling dens and announcing that all will go to hell unless they repent. Cardinal, they have even been known to startle priests and deacons passing the time of day in the brothels, alongside some of our city noblemen.

Cardinal:  Don't start this again.

Machiavelli:  But I'll tell you the latest.

Savonarola:  I am most eager to hear.

Machiavelli:  *(To Savonarola.)* It will not be news to you, for it comes from you, from your very own preaching.

Cardinal:  Oh, what has he done now?

Machiavelli:  Friar Savonarola has urged the people of Florence to be rid of their worldly possessions; the things that they love more than God. I refer, of course, to their fine silk clothes, their jewelry, their Medici works of art - sculptures and paintings.

Cardinal:  But people love these!

Savonarola:  They love them more than God, and more that their own precious souls. These things are but vanities, empty, worthless trinkets. "Vanity of vanities", saith the Preacher, in the book of Ecclesiastes.

Cardinal:  So what would you have the people do?

Machiavelli:  They will burn them; in a huge bonfire. Why, even at this very moment untold wealth is piled up in the Piazza della Signoria, ready for the torch.

Savonarola:  You see, what could be more eloquent than for people, stirred by the Gospel, and moved to repentance, than to burn the very things that supplant what should otherwise be the love of God? This is the Lord's doing and it is wondrous in our eyes.

Cardinal:  *(With some cynicism.)* And these young evangelists, Savonarola's messengers, are the white shirts of which we spoke! Tell me, Signor Machiavelli, did you repent of your unbelief? What treasured possessions did you discard so that you might at last have reconciliation with God?

Savonarola:  Yes, I also would like to know that.

Machiavelli:  Well, on the third occasion of the white shirts well nigh hammering down my front door, I confess I gave them a chair.

Savonarola:  A chair?

Cardinal:  What, some gorgeous antique, upholstered with Chinese silk, stuffed with the softest wool, and carved by the most skilled turners?

Savonarola:  That would indeed be indicative of a change of heart.

Machiavelli:  *(Dryly.)* It was an old kitchen chair for which I had no further use. But the white shirts went away happy, and thereafter left me in peace.

Savonarola:  I don't think that's the right spirit at all.

Machiavelli:  *(Warming to his rhetoric.)* And no more
is it the right spirit to fill the minds of children with
religious cant, against which they can offer no defense
because they do not have the intellectual and critical
tools to rebut what you teach them! If I were so minded
I might add that this is a corruption of children almost
as bad as that of the priests.

> *Savonarola advances on Machiavelli as if to*
> *beat him with his cane. The Cardinal gets*
> *between them.*

Cardinal:  *(Sternly.)* Stop it! Both of you! You,
Machiavelli, astound me! You, the reputed man of
moderation, with such an outburst of intemperance.

Savonarola:  I knew his heart anyway. He does not
offend me. We just see things differently. When Isaiah
says "a little child shall lead them," and the Psalmist
says "out of the mouth of babes and sucklings thou hast
perfected strength," I feel nothing but peace with what
I've done.

Machiavelli:  But you get my point, do you, that it's so
easy to fill people's minds with nonsense which they
then believe to be true? It's a kind of conspiracy of lies.
*(Posturing.)* If they believe it then I'll believe it too!

Savonarola:  In some cases, yes! And by this plain
stupidity of people who cannot think comes the very
corruption of our public life... even here in Florence.

Machiavelli:  I fear this tissue of nonsense will be with
us for many years to come. Why even this very
afternoon I saw a fine painting by Sandro Botticelli cast
upon your bonfire of the vanities.

Savonarola:  And was the subject of the painting a fair maiden, scantily clad, naked, shall we say, suffice for a thin veil?

Machiavelli:  I saw that, amongst other fine pictures and furniture.

Cardinal:  I think I could have allowed myself to take that for my own collection. Botticelli is a great artist.

Machiavelli:  You know, dealers from France, and Spain, have offered to buy many of these vanities rather than see them burnt. Then the money could be given for the completion of the Duomo. No?

Savonarola:  You mock, both of you, in your own ways. But God is not mocked. All of us will one day face the Judge of all men, at which time repentance will be too late and the mockers will only catch a glimpse of the glory of God, from afar, as they tumble into eternal darkness.

*Suddenly we hear a crackling sound, as of fire. It grows louder, and the red/orange light of a fire flickers across the faces of the three men.*

Machiavelli:  By God! They've lit the fire!

*They rush to the balustrade of the balcony and gaze down on the street.  The firelight flickers with greater intensity and the sound of burning increases. They draw back in awe, shielding their faces from the heat.*

There goes the Botticelli!

Savonarola:  And the fine robes with which women flaunt their sexuality and inveigle their ways into the beds of men.

Cardinal:  And the gambling tables. Even holy vestments torn from the churches! *(Turning angrily upon Savonarola.)* You unleashed this on Florence. This is your doing!

> *But Savonarola is in his own world. He still watches the fire, with a huge grin of satisfaction on his face, looking almost demented. Slowly the fire and the sounds subside. A clock strikes.*

Machiavelli:  Good Friar, in spite of our differences, I still count you as a friend. I have watched as you have swayed the public conscience of Florence with your wisdom and passion. You have helped subdue great violence, persuaded the King of France not to brutalize our city, and stood up to the corruption of Rodrigo Borgia, the present Pope, Alexander VI.

Cardinal:  *(A sinister note.)* And in your refusal to bow to his holiness, you have laid the kindling for yet another fire that may be more than ever you could contemplate.

Savonarola:  No. Speak the words if you must. But I have contemplated everything you have said, and far more besides. I will never deny my God, his word or my own conscience. I have said and done only what he bade me do. And I would count it my finest hour to be a martyr with all the holy men and women who have ever stood their ground against tyranny and evil.

Machiavelli:  The storm clouds are building. Trouble is brewing in the City. And you won't call off the white shirts?

Savonarola:  They are God's children doing God's work.

Machiavelli:  Then we've reached an impasse.

Savonarola:  Perhaps not.

Cardinal:  But perhaps so. You are incorrigible, Friar Savonarola. Quite unmovable.

Savonarola:  *(Smiling.)* Like a rock! The rock of Saint Peter.

> *The fire rekindles a blaze and flickers once more over the scene. This is sustained to the end of the play. There is a long pause as each contemplates where the future might lead.*

Machiavelli:  *(Softly.)* I saw you gazing into the embers of the fire. What did you see?

Savonarola:  *(With a brief shudder.)* I saw a martyr, and caught a glimpse of glory beyond.

> *The men move together, slowly, such that Machiavelli, clearly distressed, lowers his head, one hand on his forehead. The Cardinal, out of pity, places a hand on the shoulder of Savonarola, who, in turn looks upwards, and smiles. A moment. Lights fade to black.*

**_End of play._**

# Goodnight, Joe

By

John Bolen

**John Bolen** is a novelist/playwright/actor living in Southern California. His full-length play *A Tangled Affair* was included in the New Works Festival, October, 2021, at the Morgan-Wixson Theatre, Santa Monica, CA. He has been published by *Applause Theatre & Cinema Books* three times *(Hal Leonard Publishing), Independentplay(w)rights, Indigo Rising, Scars Publications, The Write Place at the Write Time, OC180news, Eunoia Review* and *YouthPLAYS*. John's plays have been produced in theatres throughout the U.S. including: New Jersey Repertory; STAGEStheatre, CA; Chance Theater, CA; Cabrillo Playhouse, CA; Theatre@First, MA; NewGate Theatre, RI; Newport Theatre Arts Center, CA; Thalian Hall Studio Center, NC; Costa Mesa Playhouse, CA; Secret Rose Theatre, CA; The Asylum Theatre, CA; Lincoln Square Theatre, Chicago, IL; Malibu Stage Company, CA; Vanguard Theatre, CA; Garden Grove Playhouse, CA; Red Room Theatre, NYC; Gallery Theatre, CA; Stage Door Repertory Theatre, CA; and the Empire Theatre, CA. His short story collection ***Nothing for Christmas & Other Holiday Tales*** and his novel ***Aurelia's Magic*** are available on Amazon. As an actor, John has worked on stage, in film and TV, and has recorded 35 books on CD. John is the Vice-President of the New Voices Playwrights Theatre & Workshop.

## CHARACTERS

Joe, male, 35

Connie, male, 32, a person with intellectual disability

> *Joe is putting down a blanket and pillow beside a bed that is center stage.*

Connie:  *(Off.)* I can't brush, Joe.

Joe: Why?

Connie:  *(Off.)* My toothbrush isn't here.

Joe: Connie, I just bought you a new one this morning. It's right there on the sink.

Connie: *(Off.)* My toothbrush is purple, Joe.

Joe:  What does it matter, Connie?  It's right there. It hasn't even been unwrapped.

Connie: *(Off.)* My toothbrush is purple.

Joe: Come on, Connie. I'll get you a purple one tomorrow. Just use the one I bought.

Connie: *(Enters.)* My toothbrush is purple, Joe.

Joe: Alright. Alright! Hey, it's okay... tomorrow, huh.

Connie: I can sleep on the floor, Joe.

Joe: Hey, that's okay. I've slept on a lot worse things than a floor. Hell, it's only for one night. Besides, it's good for my back.

> *Connie jumps on the bed.*

Connie: I like to be good for your back, Joe.

Joe: Thanks, Connie.

Connie: You can sleep on the bed tomorrow night. Then it would be good for my back.

Joe: Naw, I'm going to be taking off.

Connie: Why?

Joe: Because it's over.

Connie: But you could...

Joe: I've made up my mind.

Connie: What's going to happen to me?

Joe: I've gotta talk to Grandmama about that.

Connie: Oh. *(Pause.)* This is like camping. I liked camping.

Joe: Geez, that was so long ago. I liked camping, too. Do you remember that?

Connie: You didn't like the bugs.

Joe: No, I didn't like the bugs. Well, let's turn out the light. It's been a long day.

Connie: Joe?

Joe: Yeah, Connie.

Connie: Grandmama's bed smells funny.

Joe: Yeah, it does. The blankets have all been in mothballs.

Connie: Grandmama smells funny, too.

Joe: Yeah, she does. Maybe she's been in mothballs, too.

Connie: Do they do that?

Joe: No, it's a joke, Connie. Just a joke.

Connie: She does smell funny.

Joe: Well, goodnight.

Connie: *(Pause.)* Joe?

Joe: Yeah, Connie.

Connie: It was pretty today, wasn't it?

Joe: Jeez, Connie, I've never heard anyone describe a funeral as pretty.

Connie: There were flowers, and everyone was dressed up. People say flowers are pretty.

Joe: Yeah, Connie, flowers are pretty.

Connie: Why are flowers pretty?

Joe: What?

Connie: Why are flowers pretty?

Joe: Jeez, Connie, I don't know. I guess all the colors are nice, and they're soft and curvy.

Connie: Was Uncle Marty's tie pretty?

Joe: No, Uncle Marty's tie was definitely not pretty. And I'm certain that paisley is not ready for a comeback.

Connie: I didn't think it was pretty. *(Pause.)* Is Heaven pretty, Joe?

Joe: Yeah, I'm sure it's pretty there.

Connie: Then Heaven must not be paisley.

Joe: Yes, Connie, I'm certain that Heaven's not paisley.

Connie: Does Papa get to go to Heaven?

Joe: I sure wished him to the other place lots of times. But, I guess he was a good man; cranky as all get-out, but a good man. Yeah, he'll get to go to Heaven. Come on, let's go to sleep now.

Connie: *(Long pause.)* Joe?

Joe: Yeah, Connie.

Connie: Are you going to die now?

Joe: Jeez, Connie! What makes you say something like that?

Connie: Well, when you left you said, "I'll die before I even set foot back here again."

Joe: Damn, Connie! You can't even remember where you live, but you remember every word I said ten years ago?

*Connie sits up and starts crying.*

Connie: I only got lost once, Joe. I only got lost once.

*Joe comes up to comfort Connie.*

Joe: Hey, come on Connie, don't cry. It's alright, man. It's alright. I get lost all the time myself.

Connie: *(Wiping his eyes.)* You do?

Joe: All the time.

Connie: So are you going to die now?

Joe: No, I'm not going to die. That's just something I said in anger.

Connie: Good, 'cause I don't want you to die, Joe.

Joe: Thanks, Connie.

Connie: Why did you get angry at Papa?

Joe: I've been thinking about that a lot, ever since I heard he was sick. I was living in this little town, and I was just going nowhere. And I blamed him. I was wrong, 'cause it was my own damn fault. And I wanted to tell him and I was going to, but he died before I could get here.

Connie: If Papa goes to Heaven, maybe he can hear you.

Joe: I sure wish that.

Connie: So, you went somewhere?

Joe: Yeah, I went somewhere. But it didn't take long to figure out I was I going nowhere there, too.

Connie: If you're going nowhere anyway, maybe you could do it with me?

Joe: Geez, Connie, I'm not able to take on that kind of...

Connie: You can't leave me here, Joe.

Joe: Grandmama has a nice house here; you would have this room.

Connie: She's old, Joe.

Joe: Yeah, but...

Connie: Old people die. And then I won't have anyone.

Joe: I'd always make sure you were taken care of.

Connie: Let me go with you? I won't be any trouble. I'll brush my teeth, and I can choose my own clothes, and I won't get lost...

Joe: I haven't got much to...

Connie: All I need is you, Joe. All I need is you.

Joe: Alright, alright. I'll work it out somehow.

Connie: And then I wouldn't have to be lonely.

Joe: No, Connie, you won't ever have to be lonely. Come on, let's go to sleep now.

*Joe lies back down.*

Connie: *(Even longer pause.)* Joe?

Joe: Yeah, Connie?

Connie: If you get to Heaven, do you get to be smarter?

Joe: God, I hope so.

Goodnight, Joe

Connie: Goodnight, Joe.

***End of play.***

# It's Only Words

By

Anne V. Grob

***It's Only Words*** will have its debut performance as part of the New Voices Playwrights Theatre production Summer Voices 2022.

Anne V. Grob, a member of the Dramatist Guild, studied at SCR's Playwriting Conservatory. She has produced plays in NYC's Players Theatre SPFs of 2013-2021, winning best of festival for *Hemingway At The Larchmont*, *Once Upon A Sofa*, *The Bard of MacDougal Street*, *Alexa Takes Manhattan*, and *Used Heart*. *Mouse Play* appeared in Ohlone College Playwrights Festival 2016, and *UNTITLED* placed as finalist in Heartland Theatre 10-Minute Play Festival 2016. *The Planting Moon* placed as semi-finalist in Little Black Dress Ink's National Festival of New Work and received a staged reading in Santa Barbara April 2014. For New Voices, productions of Anne's work include: *Variations On A Composition In Blue* (Summer 2014), *How To Have A Kosher Christmas* (Holiday 2014), *The Trouble With Art* (Summer 2015), *Pentimento* (Summer 2016), *The Secret Chord* (Holiday 2016), *Not Even The Moon* (Summer 2017), *Some Simple Kindness* (Holiday 2017), *The XYZ Of It* (Summer 2018), *A Cup O' Kindness* (Holiday 2018), *G.O.A.T., or Who is Alexa?* (Summer 2019), and *Come Into My Heart* (Holiday 2021). Anne's plays appear in New Voices Playwrights Theatre anthologies, and *Variations On A Composition In Blue* was published in The Best American Short Plays 2013-2014.

## CHARACTERS

Cam, male, young adult, moody, lives with his mother and stepfather

Trudy, female, 40's, married to her late husband's brother, mother to Cam

Uncle Claude, male, late 40's, married to Trudy, uncle and stepfather to Cam

Dr. Gil Rosencrantz, male, 40's, psychotherapist and trusted family friend

> *At rise, we are in the parallel universe of a contemporary house in the suburbs and a castle in Denmark. At stage right, a living room with casual furniture; a sofa, coffee table with a small bowl on top, a wooden chair. At stage left, a closed door. Claude is seated on the sofa with an open newspaper held up in front of his face. He is dressed in everyday clothes except for the crown on his head. Trudy enters. She wears an apron tied around her waist, and a crown on her head as well. She paces around the room.*

Claude: What time are we eating?

Trudy: Where's Cam? I thought I heard him come in hours ago.

Claude: Isn't he in his room? Door's locked.

Trudy: (*Pounding on the door.*) Cam, are you there? Time to eat. I made your favorite dinner, fried pork and boiled potatoes.

Claude: Sounds delicious. How could the boy resist?

Trudy: He's not a boy. He's a Y-A.

Claude: He's a who wha?

Trudy: A young adult.

Claude: Then why is he still living with us?

Trudy: You know very well that it's on account of the pandemic.

Claude: Pandemic, schmandemic. That was two years ago. Shouldn't he be out on his own, or living with someone else and making them miserable?

Trudy: Claude Alfred Nielson! How can you say such a thing about my boy? Why he's your blood too, he's your very own nephew and I should think you'd take to mind his well-being, at least to honor my dead husband's memory who I'll remind you just happened to be your brother.

Claude: Aw, he was a no good-nik anyway. The onion doesn't fall far from the tree.

Trudy: Onions don't grow on trees. Oh, that reminds me, we're out of garlic, chives, shallots, and what else?

Claude: He stays in there all day; doesn't even come out to go to the loo.

Trudy: Leeks!

Claude: Trudy, can we please eat already? I'm starving.

*Trudy puts her hands on her hips and stares at Claude. Annoyed, she waves her arm at him, adjusts her crown, and turns her attention to the closed door.*

Trudy: Cam, come on out, dinner's getting cold! Aren't you hungry?

Cam: (*From behind the door.*) No!

Claude: What's a matter with that boy anyway? I've never seen him refuse food before.

Trudy: I'm so worried about him. He's been real mopey lately and spending too much time in his room.

Claude: Maybe he's love-struck.

Trudy: Why would you say that?

Claude: Dunno. But isn't there a girl he's been crushing on, the one he met down by the lake?

Trudy: Never talked to me about it.

Claude: Not the kind of thing you talk to your doting mother about. He knows that you think no girl's good enough for him.

Trudy: That's ridiculous. Doesn't he know I want to be a grandmother some day? What do you know about this girl anyways?

Claude: Geez Trudy, hold on a minute. The boy can't even find his way out of his room, and you've got him married and expecting a baby already.

Trudy: Maybe they broke up. Maybe he's pining for her. That would explain his unusual behavior.

Claude: If by unusual you mean crazy, yup, I agree.

> *Suddenly a note appears from under the door. The audience cannot see that there is a single letter written on it. Trudy picks it up.*

What's it say?

Trudy: (*Reading the note.*) I can hear you two talking about me. (*To Claude.*) You hear that Claude? Now you've made him upset.

Claude: This has gone far enough.

> *He throws down the newspaper and approaches the closed door.*

Cameron, this is your uncle speaking. You come out of that room right now.

> *Another note. Claude picks it up and reads it aloud.*

"Leave me alone. I'm reading." How do you like that Trudy, he's reading. Isn't that wonderful? He's reading. (*To the door.*) What do you read my lord?

> *No response. Trudy makes an attempt.*

Trudy: Cam, my boy. I love that you are so engrossed in your reading. Tell your mother, is it comedy, tragedy, history? What are you reading my son?

> *Another note. Trudy picks it up; reads it aloud.*

"Words, words, words." (*To Claude.*) Oh dear. What do you think it means?

Claude: Let me see that.

> *Claude grabs the note from Trudy.*

This doesn't say words, words, words! It says swords, swords, swords. (*Beat.*) Uh oh.

Trudy: No it doesn't. Let me have it.

> *Together they scrutinize the note, holding it up to the light, turning it this way and that.*

Claude: You see this swiggly line and then a sharp drop down?

Trudy: He does have a fine penmanship, doesn't he?

Claude: What are you talking about penmanship? This is really bad. We're going to have to bring in a specialist.

Trudy: What do you mean? Like a linguist?

Claude: No, like a shrink. Like we need to find out what's going on in his head.

Trudy: Oh dear.

Claude: I'll call Gil Rosencrantz. He's a trusted friend, he does this for a living and he's very good.

> *He pulls a phone out of his pocket and punches in a number.*

Hey, Gil. Claude here. Can you come over ASAP? We've got a situation here with Cam. He's barricaded in his room and won't come out. I think he may be going slightly…

> *Enter Gil Rosencrantz, carrying a notepad. Trudy removes her apron and hides it in the sofa.*

Gil: You rang?

Trudy: Gil, we're so worried. Can you help us?

> *She points to the closed door.*

Gil: Yes I can. Do you have a chair?

Claude: What are you going to do with it, break down the door?

Gil: No. I'm going to sit on it.

> *Claude brings him a wooden chair. Gil takes it and sets it down in front of the closed door. He takes out his notepad and pen. In a low voice, he speaks to Claude and Trudy.*

Now here's the plan. I'm going to do the word association game with him. I read him a word and he tells me what word it makes him think of. That will determine if he's cuckoo or not.

> *Gil speaks to Cam through the closed door.*

Cameron, this is Dr. Gil Rosencrantz. How are you doing in there? (*Beat.*) Cameron, you like word games, don't you? How about I give you a word from my list here and then you tell me what's the first word that comes to mind? (*Another beat.*) Okay, here we go.

> *Gil calls out a series of five letter words and waits for responses from Cam, but none are forthcoming. The reading of the words is occasionally interrupted by comments from Claude and Trudy.*

House, sling, arrow, pecan.

> *Trudy picks up the bowl from the coffee table and offers Gil some nuts.*

Trudy: Care for some?

> *Gil waves her away and continues with the list of words.*

Gil: Light, latte, Prada, ghost.

> *Suddenly a whoosh, a flash of light. Trudy sidles up to Claude.*

Trudy: I don't like this.

Gil: Sleep, dream, knife, sword.

Claude: I wouldn't go there if I were you.

Gil: You two keep interrupting me, and it hath made me mad.

Claude: Well it's not working, is it? He's still inside that room with no hope of coming out. At least we got him to write some notes.

Gil: Oh, I didn't know he wrote music.

Trudy: What my husband is trying to say is… Uh, dear, what were you saying?

Claude: Huh?

Trudy: Words, words. What were your exact words?

Gil: Won't you people please let me continue?

>*Claude and Trudy slump down together on the sofa.*

Okay, let's go on. Crown, rogue, roses.

Trudy and Claude: Moses supposes his toeses are roses.

Gil: Guys!

>*Suddenly another note appears from under the door. Gil picks it up and reads it aloud.*

Getting close.

>*He shrugs. Another note appears.*

It's a flower.

Claude: What is?

Gil: Shush!

>*More notes in quick succession. Peter reads them.*

Five letters…three vowels…A, I, Y.

Claude: Why is he doing this? He must be nuts! Soon he'll be pushing up daises.

*At once Cam opens the door and enters the
room. He looks disheveled except for the crown
on his head. Claude, Trudy, and Gil quickly rise
to their feet.*

Daisy, it's daisy! The <u>Wordle</u> for today is <u>daisy</u>!

*He grabs his mother's hands and they both start
jumping up and down. Claude and Gil look on
in amazement. Cam plops down on the sofa.*

Claude: He speaks.

Gil: Indeed.

Cam: Thanks guys. Thanks for your help.

*The others stand motionless, staring at Cam.*

What's for dinner?

*Lights begin to dim.*

Gil: (*To audience.*) And that was all he could be heard
to say. Except, sometimes late at night, the young
Prince could be found roaming the castle, muttering to
himself.

*Gil, Trudy, and Claude pick up all the notes
with the letters on them. Cam approaches the
audience and delivers a soliloquy.*

Cam: To play or not to play, That is the question.
Whether 'tis nobler to read a book or watch TV; take
the MCATs or join the Peace Corps; and thus by doing
so, to put the brain to a higher cause; and take arms
against a sea of fears. To sleep, perchance to dream, Or

battle with Morpheus 'til lightness appears, And breathe in another day, to play, the game, Consonants and vowels to be your pawns. A blank grid, and six rows of five squares, To try, to squint, to fight off yawns, Letters guessing at words till all appear in boxes of green, And what of the double letter, as yet unseen, That hath hidden its twin in between, Ay, there's the rub, To play or not to play, To sleep or not to sleep, To dream. And as darkness yields to light of dawn, The milkman cometh, and the morning paper too, Do you stretch and roll and yawn, And welcome in the newness of day? Or do you idle your day away, Until once more it's time to play?

> *Gil, Trudy, and Claude throw the notes out into the audience as all call out.*

Gil, Trudy, Claude, Cam: Wordle, Wordle, Wordle!

> *Gil offers a final aside to the audience.*

Gil: You see folks, it was really much ado about nothing. After all, it's only words.

> *Lights fade to black as we hear a few lines from the Bee Gees song <u>Words</u>: <u>It's only words, and words are all I have to take your heart away</u>.*

**<u>*End of play.*</u>**

# The Last Episode

By

John Lane

***The Last Episode*** was first produced in July, 2012 at Stage Door Repertory Theatre, Anaheim, CA. It was directed by Geoffrey Gread and starred Harv Popick, David Rusiecki, Ivar Vasco and Karen Wray.

John Lane is a founding member and former president of New Voices Playwrights Theatre. A retired professor of computer science at California State University, Long Beach, he studied playwriting at South Coast Repertory and sitcom writing at AFI in Los Angeles. Five of his short plays have been published.  He has had approximately 40 productions of his short plays in Southern California and nationally, including six in New York City. Although most of his plays are comedies, his long one-act drama *Isosceles* was part of the OC-centric New Play Festival at Chapman University, Orange, Calif.

John Lane is also a member of the Dramatists Guild, Alliance of Los Angeles Playwrights (ALAP) and Orange County Playwrights Alliance (OCPA).

## CHARACTERS

Libby, 40s, female, head writer, very much in charge

Chad, 30s, male, writer worried about his career

Danny, 50s-60s, male, seasoned writer, knows the territory

Michael, 50s, male, actor, self-important, somewhat insecure

> *The setting is the writers' room with a large table and chairs. Stacks of scripts, notebooks, a laptop, coffee cups, etc, fill the tabletop. At rise, Danny and Chad are at the table. Danny is looking at his laptop.*

Danny: *(Looking up from the laptop.)* You know, Chad, I think Libby is seriously considering having him killed off.

Chad: We can't just kill him off. Doesn't she have to clear it with the suits?

Danny:  If it's not decided, we'll have to look for alternatives.

Chad: Why kill off Michael? A lot of things revolve around Michael.

Danny: It's a matter of money. His contract is up this year. It's up to the network suits and the producers. They have the final decision on a new deal. Michael's not irreplaceable, even though he thinks he is.

Chad: It's an ensemble show for Chrissake.

Danny: They'll make the decision on Michael's fate. It all depends on his contract negotiations and the network's plans. The show hasn't been renewed yet.

Chad: Why the Christ are the delaying the pickup? We need lead time to write episodes; to plan next year. The suits never understand that.

Danny: Chad my boy, it's all money and ratings. The suits say, "Screw the writers." For them it's budgets and audience share. They couldn't write a page of dialogue if their life depended on it.

Chad: I hate to speak up in their defense, but this is a business. Ratings-wise, the show's never ranked above number 25.

Danny: Nowadays, those network honchos look like junior accountants. I doubt if any of them is over thirty. And they're making programming decisions. Libby's meeting with them this morning. She'll have more info.

Chad: The basic problem is there's too many damn cop shows. And they schedule ours on Saturday night; the graveyard slot for network shows.

Danny: That just might save us. The bar is lower; expectations are lower in that slot.

> *Libby enters. They barely notice her as she sits down.*

Libby: Let's hunker down boys. We've got some work to do.

Chad: What's up, Libby? *(Beat.)* They're canceling?

Libby: That's still pending. Since you two are working on the season's last episode, we've got to have some contingencies.

Chad: Regarding Michael's character?

Libby: Michael has become a problem. His contract is up, and he and his agent think he's due for a raise. Michael's got this grand idea that he is absolutely essential to the show.

Danny: Essential, my ass! He plays one cop, "Dennis". Cop characters get killed, they get disabled, or they quit the force. They're expendable.

Libby: If Michael's agent goes for a big raise, we may have to eliminate his "Dennis" character, which means Michael is gone.

Chad: But we still have to write the season's final episode.

Libby: There <u>are</u> some options. If the show is renewed, we can cliff-hanger; let's say Dennis is shot and in a coma, disappears or whatever. We then have the option of having him die or not.

Danny: Which gives the network a lot of leverage with Michael's agent; he can be brought back or not.

Chad: Michael's become a pain in the ass. As the table reads, the first thing he does is count his lines. Libby: All actors do that, Chad.

Chad: He cozies up to me sometimes in the writers' room, suggesting story lines; all of which, of course, feature Dennis.

Libby: Since we brought in Peter Larkin as the new sidekick this season, Michael feels threatened. Peter's young, good-looking; not to mention a good actor. Plus, he helps our demographics in the under-35s. Those demographics might just save us.

Danny: Michael's getting a bit long in the tooth. He can't handle those chase scenes.

Libby: Canceling the show is still an option for the network. We don't have a strong position. Ratings are off. We ranked fort-two last week. Not great. Even for that killer Saturday night slot.

Chad: Shit, we all might be out on the street I'd better make some plans.

Libby: Here's the deal; we have three episodes left in the season. For the final episode, we'll write two versions. One with the Dennis character possibly dead, or out of the picture. That's still the cliff-hanger option. He may or may not survive,

Danny: And that outcome largely depends on Michael's agent.

Chad: And if the show is cancelled?

Libby: Then we write a big final episode and go out it style! Wind up some of the story lines. Maybe end with a big shootout. Dennis dies, someone else dies maybe everyone dies. Maybe only Peter Larkin's Character is left standing. Maybe they'll do a spinoff with him; a whole new show around Matt.

Chad: And maybe save our jobs.

Danny: Don't forget. Writers are expendable, too.

Libby: Boys, let's get on it now. Let's do some brainstorming. Our outline for the last episode has Dennis and Matt investigating some smuggling by the Russian mafia; smuggling illegal Chinese immigrants. Maybe some chase scenes in squad cars or a boat chase.

Danny: Let's put in a foot chase so Dennis has to do some running. You know how Michael hates chase scenes.

Chad: Danny, you're cruel.

Danny: Maybe he has to climb over a fence. He despises that.

Chad: Why does there always have to be a fence?

Danny: If a cop is chasing a perp on foot, as some point he has to climb over a fence. I think it's written in stone somewhere. *(Beat.)* I know Michael hates those scenes, but he's such a pompous jerk, I purposely write them in.

Chad: You are very, very cruel, Danny.

Libby: Let's focus guys. Think about the last episode of the series option; the "we just got cancelled" version.

> *Michael enters.*

Michael: Hi, guys. Hi, Libby.

Libby: Michael, what are you doing here? We're pretty busy. You shouldn't be in the writers' room.

Michael: Had a meeting upstairs. Thought I'd drop in. Season's winding up; wanted to take a look at the upcoming episodes.

Libby: We're working on the last three. Chad and Danny here are working on the last one.

Danny: How are your negotiations going, Michael? Sort of down to the wire, aren't they?

Michael: My agent's handling it. I try not to get involved with that contract stuff.

Libby: No agreement on terms yet?

Michael: They're trying to work it out. I don't want to be greedy.

Chad: of course not.

Michael: Although the show's been doing pretty well.

Libby: Not that well. We ranked 42$^{nd}$ last week.

Michael: *(Pause.)* To be frank, there've been rumblings about cancelling the show; all that scuttlebutt. The show's got a following. Cancelling would be a big mistake. I put my heart and soul into that show.

Chad: We'd all like to save the show, Michael. Bringing in Peter Larkin has been an asset.

Michael: Hmm, Peter's sort of a pretty boy type. *(Beat.)* Don't get me wrong; he's a nice kid but I'm not sure if he has the acting chops.

Libby: He does bring a younger demographic to the show.

Danny: And Peter handles the action scenes pretty well.

Michael: Action scenes are overrated. This is a procedural cop show. We're detectives. We follow leads; we interview witnesses; we wear business suits for Chrissake. Do we need all those damn chase scenes? If I have to climb another chain-link fence, or go down another fire escape, I'll...

Libby: ...Actually, we're writing Peter into more of those. He's more athletic.

Danny: Possibly emphasize Peter's character a bit more.

Michael: Well, we shouldn't upset the balance of the show. Though I suppose we could try to...

Chad: ...We all want the series to be picked up. We have to do what it takes.

Libby: Bottom line, Michael, if the network decides to cancel the show, we need to have a final episode ready; something to bring closure to the series; tie up the loose ends.

Michael: Have you thought about a cliff-hanger? That might bring the audience back next fall. Remember the old "Dallas" series and "Who Shot J.R."?

Libby: We thought about it. The cliff-hanger has to involve one of the main characters. That would be you or Peter or both of you.

Michael: I get it. We've gone missing, or whatever; possibly dead. But we turn up safe in the first fall episode. That could mean boffo ratings.

Danny: If we get picked up. Getting renewed is all about budget and ratings.

Libby: Contract renewals can definitely affect the cost per episode. It's a big factor.

Michael: I guess it's no secret that my agent is looking for a bump in my contract. But I wouldn't want to be greedy.

Chad: As you said before.

Michael: Agents like to play hardball.

Danny: Maybe this is not the year to play hardball.

Michael: As long as I'm here, maybe we could talk over some other script ideas.

Chad: For the cliff-hanger?

Libby: We were considering a chase, maybe a boat chase in the harbor. We haven't done a boat chase before. It would be something involving the Russian mafia smuggling Chinese immigrants inside cargo ships.

Michael: I like it! A boat chase; and that wouldn't involve any running.

Danny: Then some kind of big collision; destroys the police boat. Let's say they find the wreckage, but Dennis and Matt are missing.

Libby: Yeah, both of you would be missing, presumed drowned or dismembered.

Michael: Great! Then next season, in the first episode, they discover we've been picked up by a yacht or a fishing boat. *(Beat.)* Wow! Ratings through the roof!

Libby: That's one scenario.

Danny: Or one of you swims to safety.

Michael: Only one? *(Warily.)* Which one would that be?

Chad: Logically speaking, Peter's character Matt is younger, more fit. He would presumably have the stamina to swim to safety.

Michael: Dennis could cling to some wreckage. Then some fishing boat rescues me. Maybe I'd have amnesia from the accident; can't remember who I am.

Libby: This is a cop show, Michael, not a soap opera. Cops don't get amnesia.

Michael: Those location scenes in the harbor, they could be expensive; the explosions, the wreckage, the stunts, all that. Maybe something cheaper?

Danny: I got one; you're in pursuit, you're over-exerting yourself, let's say, trying to climb a chain-link fence. And you have a heart attack.

Michael: Another damn fence?

Chad: They bring Dennis to the E.R., he needs a quintuple bypass; it's touch and go. Maybe he's left on life support indefinitely or he could be confined to a wheel chair for the rest of his life.

Michael: Hmm. That might work. Remember Raymond Burr in that old show "Ironside". He was chief of detectives and was in a wheelchair for the entire series.

Chad: "Ironside"? Never heard of it.

Michael: Are you young guys completely out of touch with the 70s? The golden age of cop shows; "Streets of San Francisco", "Kojak"...

Danny: ..."Rockford Files", "Hawaii Five-0"...

Libby: Don't forget "Police Woman" you sexist bastards.

Chad: "Hawaii Five-0" is back again. Not a bad show. I wonder if the writers get to stay in Hawaii.

Libby: Let's talk turkey here, Michael. It's possible your character Dennis dies.

Michael: But Dennis is the pivotal character. He has a following.

Libby: There's no pivotal character. It's an ensemble show, Michael: a cop show. Think about "Law and Order"; how many cast changes did they go through. The show survived.

Danny: A lot of those cast changes were based on contract disputes. I'd bet money on it. Being a cop is dangerous. Cops can get killed in the line of duty. Cops have a high suicide rate.

Michael: Our characters Dennis and Matt have a nice chemistry. Shame to break it up.

Libby: Let's talk about the other option.

Chad: The final episode option; when the show is cancelled. No need for a cliff-hanger.

Danny: We go out in style.

Michael: Yes, but no one gets killed. We all live for another day, a final episode... with some good writing, good acting... might get us an Emmy nomination. If we do it right, that episode could be the audition for a new show; maybe a spin-off. My Dennis character could be a private detective; takes on cases involving missing children.

Libby: We all have a stake in putting out a good final episode. Good writing is in demand.

Chad: That episode is our calling card. *(Thinks.)* Hmm. Maybe get on staff for "Hawaii Five-0". I'd love to live in Hawaii; the weather, the chicks, the surfing.

Libby: We want a "noble" final episode, Michael; maybe your character dies rescuing a family of Chinese immigrants. We fade out on a big police funeral.

Danny: *(Sees it.)* Cemetery scene: long motorcycle procession, bagpipes, the whole thing.

Michael: I don't like funerals. Frankly, I'd prefer the wheelchair option. Not quite so final.

Chad: Better yet, suppose we follow the Russian mafia scenario. The last scene's in a courtroom. The D.A. has won the case against the Russians. You and the D.A., in court, walking down the aisle at the end of the trial. Justice has been served.

Michael: Then maybe a scene in front of the courthouse. All the press rushing towards Dennis; cameras; microphones. But I shoo them off. I push through and just walk away from the mob. *(Holds his hands up to frame the imaginary shot.)* I see a wide angle crane shot, slowly pulling up and back as I walk away... alone.

Danny: Peter's character would have to be there, too, somehow.

Libby: Maybe Peter's character and yours walk in opposite directions.

Michael: Then a spin-off; a new show with Dennis again, let's say, as an arson investigator.

Chad: Or a spin-off with Peter. He's got a following.

Michael: Peter's a good-looking kid, but let's face it, he just doesn't have the... gravitas.

Libby: I'm not sure the 18-to-34-demographic cares about gravitas, Michael. And Peter doesn't cost that much. I think they signed him pretty cheap.

Michael: *(Pause.)* Maybe I could make some adjustments. I could call my agent.

> *Libby's cell phone rings. She picks up and answers.*

Libby; Yeah, Mortie... yeah, we considered that... we thought about a cliff-hanger, but... you want just a normal episode... nothing grand. Gotcha.

*Libby hangs up the phone.*

Danny: So, what's the deal?

Libby: Mortie wants a garden-variety episode; no cliff-hanger, no big finish. He knows we need lead time to write the last episode. We're over budget for the season. I guess that means no boat chase; nothing grandiose. We need something low budget. No stunts.

Michael: No fucking fences.

Danny: This way all options are still there. If they pull the plug, then this episode will be the last. No fanfare. The series dies an uneventful death; goes out with a whimper, noted only *(Gesturing with his fingers.)* by a small paragraph in "Variety".

Chad: I wonder if it's expensive to live in Hawaii if I could get a gig on that show.

Libby: Or... we can still get picked up. The network suits are looking at the numbers; ratings, cost-per-episode, demos. Nothing is a done deal.

Danny: Yeah, those young accountant punks in dark suits run the numbers on their iPads, iPods, or whatever. They probably would've dropped "Kojak" after its first three episodes because they didn't like the demographics.

Michael: *(Pause.)* You guys do know that I love the show. I hope that's clear. I love you writers. I love the cast. I love my Dennis character. *(Beat.)* I go in restaurants or to supermarkets and people say, "What's up, Dennis?" I like that recognition.

Libby: We all like the show, Michael. We'd all like another season.

> *After a long pause, Michael slowly takes out his cell phone and punches a number.*

Michael: Hi, Marie, put me through to Max will you.

Chad: *(To Libby.)* Who's Max?

Libby: His agent.

Michael: Max, you know that figure we were looking at the other day? Let's scale it down a bit... Maybe scale it down a bit more. In fact, I could live with the current contract if push comes to shove.

Chad: *(Aside to the others.)* And push <u>has</u> definitely come to shove.

Michael: *(Still on his cell phone.)* Yeah, for the good of the show. *(Pause.)* Yeah, Max, that's what I want. *(He hangs up.)*

Libby: You took one for the team, Michael.

Chad: Although we still haven't been renewed.

Libby: I'm more optimistic than you guys. I think we might get another season. Let's get writing.

Michael: Just one thing. Let Peter do those chase scenes. He's young, he's athletic and he looks great in those tight suits Women will eat him up.

Libby: *(Beat.)* Okay, boys, get on your laptops and finish that last episode. No Harbor chase, no explosions, no Russians and no cliff-hanger.

Michael: How about "no fence climbing for Dennis"? That's a reasonable request.

Danny: Yeah, why not? We owe you one, Michael. No fences.

*Blackout.*

**_End of play._**

# Power Hour

By

David Rusiecki

David Rusiecki is the president of the New Voices Playwrights Theatre. A member since 2009, he has contributed to New Voices Playwrights Theatre as a writer, director, actor and co-producer. He has also served as head of the New Works Festival Literary Committee and Board of Trustees with the Long Beach Playhouse. His full-length *Sides* was selected for the Long Beach Playhouse New Works table-read series while in the same year *...Prep...* received honorable mention with Panndora Productions' annual festival of new play readings. His one-act play *Kid Gloves* (originally entitled *Have A Nice Day*) has been published in **The Best American Short Plays 2012-2013** (Applause Books) as well as in **Best Monologues from Best American Short Plays** (Applause Books). His one-act play *Long Time Coming* has been published in **The Best American Short Plays 2014-2015** (Applause Books). Other one-act plays produced by New Voices Playwrights Theatre include *Mistle-in-Tow* at STAGEStheatre (Fullerton, CA) along with *Two-Some*, *A Fake Christmas*, *The Big 3-0*, *$ecret $anta*, *Long Time Coming*, *Holiday Hoo-Ha*, *Return To Sender*, *Have A Nice Day*, and *Last Call* at Stage Door Repertory Theatre (Anaheim, CA). Other full-length works which received staged readings include *Groupie* at Theatre Out (Santa Ana, CA) as well as *Scattered Showers*, *The Wrecking Ball* and *Goon* at Stage Door Repertory Theatre. He can be reached at: djrusiccki@gmail.com

## CHARACTERS

Reza, early 60s, male

Brooke, early 20s, female

> *Lights rise on a dining table at a public restaurant. We see Reza sitting alone reading a menu. He wears a casual outfit. Brooke enters, wearing a face mask, latex gloves, black dress shirt, blue jeans, black slip-on shoes and a black apron. Pens, receipts and a notepad jut out of the apron sleeve. She hurries past him who waves for her attention.*

Reza: Excuse me?

> *She stops in her tracks and turns to him, annoyed.*

Reza: I'd like to put my order in.

Brooke: Okaaay...

> *She inches toward the table, pulling down her face mask.*

Would you like to start out with some wine? We have this special promotion celebrating and supporting Empowering Women Together in partnership with a non-profit winery in the Yakima Valley region of Washington. With each glass purchased, an economic contribution will be donated to this charitable organization. We have three distinct wines: a Rose, a Sauvignon Blanc and a bold Red Blend.

Reza: No, no... no thank you, I'm not interested in any of that.

Brooke: Okay then, what can I get you?

Reza: Don't you need to write this down?

Brooke: I have stellar recall.

Reza: No, no... I want you to write down my order so you don't make a mistake.

Brooke: I don't need to, I'm good.

Reza: Please, I insist.

*She begrudgingly pulls out her notepad and pen.*

Brooke: Would you like to start out with some water?

Reza: I'd like an iced tea to drink.

Brooke: We're out of iced tea.

Reza: Can't you brew some more?

Brooke: Um, no... I'm afraid we can't.

Reza: How come?

Brooke: Like I said, we're all out of iced tea. We're waiting to get a new shipment this week.

Reza: Oh, how about lemonade?

Brooke: We finished our last batch of lemonade too.

Reza: I don't believe this. Never mind then, can you tell me what comes with the Chicken Parmesan?

Brooke: Kale.

Reza: I'm sorry?

Brooke: The Chicken Parmesan comes with Kale Salad and pine nuts.

Reza: Oh, I don't care for any of that. What's the soup of the day?

Brooke: Our Signature Homemade Soup today is Chicken Tomatillo.

Reza: Chicken-what?

Brooke: Chicken Tomatillo.

Reza: What's that like?

Brooke: It's made with tomatillos, onion, jalapenos, lime and cilantro. Sort of like a Mexican chicken noodle soup but spicy.

Reza: It's spicy?

Brooke: Yeah.

Reza: How spicy?

Brooke: Um, pretty darn spicy.

Reza: This soup you have... Chicken, what do you call it again?

Brooke: Chicken Tomatillo?

Reza: I'll have a bowl.

Brooke: But we're out of that too.

Reza: I'm sorry?

Brooke: We're out of Chicken Tomatillo.

Reza: How can you be out of all these items?

Brooke: Um... because like, the kitchen closes in five minutes and we've served all those dishes to customers who arrived earlier in the day.

Reza: Never mind, I'll have a cup of the Tomato Basil soup.

Brooke: We're out of that too.

Reza: What?

Brooke: We're out of Tomato Basil soup. We do have Lobster Bisque.

Reza: No, no... I don't like Lobster Bisque. Listen, I don't have time. I'll have the Grilled Flat-Iron Steak, medium well.

Brooke: We're also out of steaks.

Reza: That's impossible.

Brooke: Our chef eighty-sixed our last steak on the menu half-an-hour ago.

Reza: Well what do you have left?

Brooke: Lobster Bisque.

Reza: You told me that already. What else?

Brooke: Um, that's about it.

Reza: That's all you have? Lobster Bisque? That's impossible. I'll have an espresso then.

Brooke: We don't do espressos. Specialty coffees are served downstairs at our Coffee Bar on the second floor.

Reza: You don't do espressos here?

Brooke: We serve only regular and decaf coffee.

Reza: I'll take a decaf.

Brooke: We're out of decaf.

Reza: This is completely unacceptable.

Brooke: I'm terribly sorry.

Reza: Why it is like this every time I come here. You're out of this item; you're out of that item.

Brooke: Well, probably because you come during Power Hour.

Reza: I'm sorry?

Brooke: Power Hour. That's our last hour before the kitchen closes.

Reza: So?

Brooke: That's when we try our very best to get rid of everything and serve everyone before we're done for the day.

Reza: That doesn't make a difference. You should have these items.

Brooke: You're absolutely right, I agree.

Reza: And you shouldn't be closing a six pm. You should stay open at least until nine o'clock.

Brooke: That's a terrific suggestion. I'll pass that along to management. Anything else I can get you?

Reza: At this point, I don't know what I want. Tell me, what can you give me?

Brooke: Not much, we got hit pretty good earlier today. How about a Simple Salad?

Reza: Simple Salad?

Brooke: Yes.

Reza: Anything else?

Brooke: Maybe some of the Starters like... Cilantro Lime Chicken Tacos.

Reza: I don't want that.

Brooke: Okay, then there's also the Heirloom Tomatoes and Burrata.

Reza: What's Burrata?

Brooke: It's an Italian cheese made with mozzarella and cream.

Reza: Is it good?

Brooke: The Burrata? Yes, it's very popular with our appetizers.

Reza: I guess... I guess then I'll take that.

Brooke: All-right, one Heirloom Tomato Burrata...anything else?

Reza: Well, I don't know. What's the Chef's Featured Pizza?

Brooke: Oooh, the Chef's Featured Pizza is Prosciutto and Arugula.

Reza: Fine, I'll have that.

Brooke: That's been eighty-sixed as well.

Reza: What kind of an operation is this? I need to speak to your manager.

Brooke: Okaaay, but it's gonna be a wait. She's kinda busy right now in the kitchen expediting requests.

Reza: I don't understand.

Brooke: You see, our expo had to leave early so she's covering for him.

Reza: What does that have to do with...

Brooke: She's making sure all the kitchen orders are prepared in an orderly fashion.

Reza: Is it always like this here? I had to wait forty-five minutes outside before I could be seated.

Brooke: No, it's not always like this. We're usually a lot more organized. But, you see since COVID...we're not fully staffed. We have limited seating capacity which explains your wait.

Reza: Your hostess should have told me that.

Brooke: I find that hard to believe. She and I are very close friends. In fact, I got her the job and I know for a fact she tells every guest that kitchen is about to close. She gives every guest a copy of the menu and personally recommends they know what they want ahead of time. If it were up to me, personally I'd stop dining service at five o'clock and make all food requests To-Go. The kitchen crew has family members at home waiting for them just like you do, I'm sure. And they very much would like to go home and cook for them. So while we're stretched a little thin as a staff... we're also doing our best to please our customers. Next time, I suggest you arrive early and not five minutes to close so we can properly assist you.

*He stares at her.*

Reza: Okay, I'll have the Lobster Bisque.

Brooke: Cup or a bowl?

Reza: I'll have a cup.

Brooke: Would you like some bread rolls to go with it?

Reza: How much are bread rolls?

Brooke: They're free.

Reza: Okay... thanks.

Brooke: You're very welcome. I'll be right back. I can take your menu if you like.

*He hands her the menu. She exits leaving him sitting alone. A few moments later, she returns with a bowl of soup. She places it in front of him. She watches him take a sip.*

Brooke: So?

Reza: A little better this time. I like how you pushed the wine promotion in the beginning. That's a good way to start.

Brooke: Okay.

Reza: Please sit down and I'll give you the rest of your performance review.

**<u>End of play.</u>**

# Sensitivity Training 101

## By

## John Franceschini

***Sensitivity Training 101*** will have its debut performance as part of the New Voices Playwrights Theatre production Summer Voices 2022.

John Franceschini is a playwright living in Southern California.  He has been published by *Applause Theatrebooks* and *New Voices Playwrights Theatre.* John's plays have been produced at: City Theatre of Independence, MO; St. Johnsbury Academy, MA; Simpson College, IA; The Theatre at Hollywood and Vine, MA; Starlite Players, FL; Vienna Theatre Company, VA; Paw Paw Village Players, MI; The Globe Theatre, TX; Spokane Radio Theatre, WA; West Coast Players, FL; Pend Orielle Playhouse Community Theatre, WA; Stage Door Productions, VA; Downers Grove North High School, IL; Wasatch Theatre Company, UT; Wells College, NY; Holton-Arms High School, MD, Madison Central High School, KY; Carroll College, MT, Bradley Playhouse, Conn; Stage Left Theatre, WA.  In California at: Harvard Street Theatre Company; SkyPilot Theatre; Lonny Chapman Theatre; Found Theatre; Ohlone College; Three Roses Players; Theatre Out; Stage Door Repertory Theatre; Cabrillo Playhouse; STAGEStheatre; Mysterium Theater; and Empire Theatre.

John is a member of: Dramatist Guild of America, New Voices Playwrights Theatre and Orange County Playwrights Alliance.

<u>Characters</u>

Doctor Margaret Merrill, female, 30s, a psychologist with an amiable, upbeat mood.  She runs the 'Sensitivity Training Center'. She helps clients attain behavioral improvement.

Destiny, female, 20s, a bit of a free spirit.  She has a low flash point with anger management.  She lives more in her feelings and emotions.  She has residual psychological baggage.

Mark, male, 20s, a trained actor who does Improv and works at the Sensitivity Center role-playing in various 'case scenarios' with clients.

> *Suggested room with a table and one chair.  A sign on the wall reads, Sensitivity Training Center. At rise, Doctor Merrill, wearing a white lab coat, is standing and reading a document in a manila folder. Her cell phone buzzes.  She answers.*

Dr. Merrill: Oh, good, she's here.  Please send her in.

> *Destiny enters.*

Dr. Merrill: *(Bubbly.)* Hello Destiny, and welcome to the *Sensitivity Training Center*.  We're delighted to have you here. My name is Doctor Margaret Merrill, but please call me Doctor Maggie.  I think a bit of informality helps raise our trust level.  Don't you think?

Destiny: Dr. Maggie, I haven't been sleeping too well. I could use some downers to knock me out.

Dr. Merrill: Heavens no, I don't write prescriptions. I'm a psychologist, I'll assist you in strengthening your interpersonal skills with customers at your firm.

Destiny: How about a swig of whiskey?  I've heard big shots at these companies keep a bottle in their desk for happy hour.  I could use something to smooth out the rough edges.

Dr. Merrill: You do look a bit peaked 'around the gills', so to speak.  But sorry, nothing stronger than caffeinated coffee on the premises.

Destiny: We do break for lunch, don't we?  I saw a bar across the street.

Dr. Merrill: Destiny, you have an exciting day ahead of you.  You'll discover new learnings which can be applied to your 'customer service' interactions at your firm.

Destiny*: (Lackluster.)* My boss told me to be here at nine o' clock.  So here I am.

Dr. Merrill: That's the spirit!  An enthusiastic outlook will serve you well and shine through to co-workers and customers alike.

Destiny: I don't even know why my company sent me here.  What's this all about?

> *Doctor Merrill pulls a document from the manila folder.*

Dr. Merrill: Your Human Resources department wants us to work on… how shall we say this… anger management issues.

Destiny: I don't have any deficiencies in that area!  This is an insult if my company thinks I'm some kind of hot head.  Who said that!  I'll rip them a new one.

Dr. Merrill: One can only benefit from incremental improvements to one's comportment.  A tweak here, a tweak there, will serve you well.

Destiny: *(Glumly.)* I did get a day out of the office so that's not too bad, I guess.

Dr. Merrill: Jolly good, keep up that positive attitude!

Destiny: Alright, what do you want me to do?

Dr. Merrill: We'll begin with an assessment of where you stand on the continuum of the 'Customer Service' scale.  Then we can design a learning program specifically for you.  Think of it like having a dress custom tailored to fit.

Destiny: I don't have a clue about what you just said.

Dr. Merrill: I may be proven incorrect but I feel like this may become an interesting day.

Destiny: Come on, let's get this show on the road.

Dr. Merrill:  Knowing your mind and speaking out forcefully is a trait we need to see more often in women these days.  Kudo to you!  *(Beat.)* I usually assign new attendees to one of our wonderfully talented trainers.  But in this instance, I think you might benefit from my guiding hand.

Destiny: Whatever you say.

Dr. Merrill: Your contagious enthusiasm just bubbles through and lifts up everyone around you!

Destiny: Do I sit here and take notes?

*Doctor Merrill uses her cell phone.*

Dr. Merrill: Please send in Mark.

*Mark enters.*

This is Mark. He's an actor and will play the role of a customer. Mark is trained in improvisation and will go with the flow. You will play the part of a salesclerk in a department store. It's called a 'scenario' and we'll do a few of these this morning.

Destiny: Oh, I see we're going to pretend.

Dr. Merrill: Amazing how quickly you catch on! *(To Mark.)* Mark, let's do *Customer Number -Three.*

*Mark approaches Destiny.*

Mark: Excuse me. How can I find the Men's Department?

Destiny: We sell nylons here. Does your girlfriend wear nylons?

Mark: Excuse me?

Destiny: Or does she show bare leg?

Mark: I'm having trouble following you.

Destiny: I can put on one of our sheerest pair. You can watch me slide them up my legs.

Mark: I want to buy some ties.

Destiny: Does that mean you do, or don't have a girlfriend?

Dr. Merrill: Time out!  Destiny, a 'point of learning' here.  We do want to give the customer a warm greeting when they enter our space.  And just out of curiosity, where did the 'nylon' thing come from?

Destiny: I need to know whether Mark has a girlfriend.

Dr. Merrill: Pray tell, why is that important, pet?

Destiny: If he has a girlfriend then I won't waste my time on him.  But if not, he's fair game.  *(Beat.)* I think Mark is handsome.

Dr. Merrill: Oh, little potato bug, this is not a dating bar.  We want to get the customer to the Men's department so he can make a purchase.  Let's regroup and do another scenario. *(To Mark.)* Mark, let's do *Customer Number-Five*.

*Mark puts on a pair of sunglasses.*

Mark: I purchased this shirt the other day.  It's the wrong size.  Would you process the return and give me a credit?

Destiny: Get away from me, you pervert, or I'll call security!

Mark:  What?

Destiny: You're undressing me with your eyes and checking out my rack!

Mark: I'm wearing sunglasses, you can't see my eyes.

Destiny: I don't have to; I can feel your eyes all over me.

Mark: That's preposterous!

Destiny: Get away from me or I'll rip an eyeball outta your face and feed it to a crow!

Mark: You're loco, lady!  I'm not buying anything in this store!  Goodbye!

Dr. Merrill: Let's take a breather here.  *(Beat.)* Destiny, little butterfly, are we associating some past emotional injury with this scenario?  If we do, we're allowing those experiences to become self-inflicting triggers for anger.  Just wipe the chalkboard clean and begin each day anew!

Destiny: If you ask any man what's the first thing he notices about a woman, he'll answer, "It depends on which way she's walking".  Men are rodents!

Doctor Merrill: You won't get an argument from me on that one.  *(Beat.)* I know someone who wore their best dress which gives just a hint of cleavage, on a first date.  And what's the guy do?  He practically leans over the table with a telescope.  Men are termites.  *(Beat.)* Oh sorry, my mind was drifting… where were we?

Density: I don't think this is working for me.

Doctor Merrill: Don't be a 'Negative Nancy'.  We're just beginning.  At the conclusion of today's session, you'll be 'as right as rain'!  *(Beat.)* I want you to use an 'anger defusing technique', in the next scenario.  Before you respond, take a series of deep breaths, inhale… exhale… inhale… exhale, then slowly count to ten.

Destiny: I can do that.  Inhale… exhale… inhale… exhale, then slowly count to ten.

Doctor Merrill: Since you raised the specter of sexual harassment in the workplace, we'll go with that.  *(To Mark.)* Mark, let's do *Customer Number-Thirteen.*

*Mark approaches Destiny.*

Mark: Yo, toots, you're one good looking broad.

Destiny: What did you say?

Mark: I came into the store to buy some shoes but, I saw you and had to come over.  I think we were made for each other.

Destiny: You do?  We don't even know one another.

Mark: It's like animal magnetism.  I can feel the electricity in the air.  Tony here, that's me, can light your Christmas Tree, know what I mean?

Destiny: I think I do.

Mark: Tony, that's me, can give you the non-stop ride of your life.

Destiny: Tony, are you married?

Mark: My wife's married, I'm not.  Whata' you say, want to come into the dressing room with me.

Destiny: Yeah, sure. Oh, don't mind the blister on me tongue, it's the size of a lemon.  The doctor said it should clear up in a couple of months.  Wanna' French-kiss?

Mark: On second thought…

Destiny: *(Quickly.)* Inhale! Exhale!... Nine… Ten. *(Beat.)* You two-timing piece of shit!  I'll tear your lungs outta your chest, mix them with eggs and have them for breakfast.

Doctor Merrill: Time out.  Destiny, my little pumpkin, we don't say the words, 'Inhale, Exhale' but actually do the breathing.  Let's process our feelings right now while they're fresh.

Destiny: It's despicable to say, "…My wife's married, I'm not…"  What a low-life scum.  Men are slugs.

Doctor Merrill: Can't argue those facts, my pet.  You're right to feel indignant. The trouble we women face seems to be due to men and yes, it's always a man. *(Beat.)* I know someone who opened her heart to a man, then wham, he finds a new 'flavor of the month' and the woman was discarded like yesterday's newspaper. All those feelings and emotions you thought meant something were tossed out the window.

Destiny: How did that make you feel?

Doctor Merrill: I hit him in the crotch, with my knee!  It was exhilarating, very cleansing.  *(Beat.)* Oh, sorry, were we talking about me?

Destiny: That's precisely how I feel when I have those outbursts.  But I want to get better and not have fits of anger.  Is it possible for me to change?

Doctor Merrill: My little caterpillar friend, we'll equip you with the tools to use to accomplish that goal. We'll get to those this afternoon. But first, we'll do one last scenario which employs 'Listening Skills'.

Destiny: What does that mean?

Doctor Merrill: Listening can help improve communication and help you avert potentially hostile emotions.

Destiny: How?

Doctor Merrill: First, you listen to what the customer says. Then you say, "Let me make sure I understand what you're saying". Then restate it back to them in your own words. This can clarify misunderstandings.

Destiny: I'll give it a try, I guess.

Doctor Merrill: It's exciting to see your continued keenness for our workshop exercises. *(To Mark.)* Mark, let's do *Customer Number-Twelve*.

> *Mark approaches Destiny. He's carrying a small bouquet of flowers.*

Mark: I'm meeting someone here soon. In the meantime, would you show me some scarves?

Destiny: Hey, I recognize you. You were in here today. I waited on you. Oh, look, you brought me some flowers. They're beautiful.

> *Destiny takes the bouquet from Mark's hand.*

Mark: Wait a minute! They're for my girlfriend!

Destiny: Hey, there's a card with the bouquet. It says, 'Rest in Peace', Henrietta. How sweet of you to think of me. Is that your nickname for me?

Mark: I found them in the cemetery; I'm going to use them as a prop at my improv club tonight.

Destiny: Yes, I'll go with you to the club.

Mark: I already have a date. There's a misunderstanding here.

Destiny: Let me restate what I understand you said to me. "Here, these flowers are for you. My nickname for you is 'Henrietta' and I'm taking you to the improv club tonight. Afterwards, we'll go to my place for first-date sex".

Mark: What was that last part?

Destiny: 'First-date sex tonight'.

Mark: Yeah, that's a perfect recap of what I said! I can pick you up tonight after your session.

Doctor Merrill: Whoa! Rein-in that stallion, cowboy! Mark, I want to talk to Destiny alone. Take a break, help another trainer

Mark: I'll see you later, Destiny.

Doctor Merrill: Destiny, my little Sugar Plum Fairy, let's huddle on this one. This isn't what I had in mind when we discussed 'listening-skills'.

Destiny: I think Mark's handsome. We might start dating. But we have to have sex first then decide on dating.

Doctor Merrill: It might be best to get to know one another first.  You know, develop findings and emotions for each other.  Then the physical act of lovemaking would have more meaning and pleasure.

Destiny: Why go through the time to get to know someone before having sex?  What if the sex isn't good?  Then you're trapped in a dead-end relationship.  See what I mean?

Doctor Merrill: Hmm, I think I do.  Once you become emotionally invested in a person it becomes much harder to end the relationship for whatever reason.

Destiny: Exactly, this way, it's like, no harm, no foul.  You each walk away without any emotional wounds.

Doctor Merrill: Well-constructed logic on your part, Destiny.  I never considered that line of thinking.  There's much food for thought there.

Destiny: You can bond all you want afterwards.  Doesn't that make more sense?

Doctor Merrill: Let me restate what I think you just said, "Jump in the sack, bang the hell out of each other, then decide if you want to take the elevator to paradise or go out and get a cheese sandwich."

Destiny: Bingo!  You're a quick learner with lots of enthusiasm, Doctor Maggie.

Doctor Merrill: I'm intrigued.  Let's take a break and go to the bar across the street.  We can discuss this in more depth over a *Bloody Mary*.

Denise: That's the best scenario yet.

*They both exit.*

**<u>End of play.</u>**

# The Tsunami Sisters

By

Fengar Gael

Fengar Gael has had readings, workshops, and productions at the Sundance Theatre Lab, Utah Shakespearean Festival, the InterAct Theatre of Philadelphia, New Jersey Repertory, Playwrights Theatre of New Jersey, Detroit Repertory Theatre, the Salt Lake Acting Company, the Moxie Theatre of San Diego, The Kitchen Dog Theatre of Dallas, The Irish Theatre of Chicago, the Botanicum Seedlings of Topanga, California, Harelquin Productions of Auburn New York, the Rorschach Theatre of D. C., the Venus Theatre of Laurel, Maryland, and in New York City: Playwrights Gallery, Urban Stages, MultiStages, the Abingdon Theatre, The Secret Theatre, The Spiral Theatre, Collaborative Arts Project 21, Turn to Flesh Productions, The Resonance Ensemble Theatre, Medicine Show Theatre, The Identity Theater, Yonder Window Theatre, and Ego Actus Theatre. She is a recipient of the Craig Noel Award (for **Devil Dog Six**), the Playwrights First Award (for **Opaline**), Manhattan Theatre Works Excellence in Playwriting Award (for **The Draper**); and commissions from South Coast Repertory, the Hangar Theatre, New Jersey Repertory and the InterAct Theatre (through the National New Play Network), and a playwriting fellowship from the California Arts Council. Enquiries should be addressed to her agent:Elaine Devlin Literary, Inc.,411 Lafayette Street (6th floor), New York, NY 10003, (212) 842-9030, elaine@edevlinlit.com

## CHARACTERS

Doctor Hannah Waverly, a Jamaican born gynecologist

Doctor Lillian Sherborn, a pregnant marine biologist

River Sherborn, Lillian's twin daughter from the fetal stage to age twelve

Rain Sherborn, Lillian's twin daughter from the fetal stage to age twelve

NOTE: River and Rain are intended to be played by young adult actors

> *The present, and twelve years earlier at Montego Bay, Jamaica. A stylized set represents a tented carnival sideshow in the present, and a parlor and pool in the past. In the spotlight of a tented sideshow, Dr. Hannah Waverly stands to address the audience, speaking with a Caribbean accent.*

Hannah:  Ladies and gentlemen: First, I must remind you that this is a carnival sideshow, not a courtroom and I am not on trial. I am told that you are a very special audience, composed entirely of scientists, many willing to live in exile and defy restrictions on research of any kind. By now we realize that no one can suppress the human quest for knowledge; not credulous clerics, not ignorant politicians, not even the president of the United States... so I appreciate your willingness to hear my side of the story. My name is Doctor Hannah Waverly. I was educated at Columbia University, and was once a practicing gynecologist here in Jamaica. Twelve years ago, Doctor Lillian Sherborn called me to her home in Montego Bay. A mutual friend assured her that I could be discreet because...

*As Hannah speaks, she approaches Dr. Lillian Sherborn standing in her parlor.*

Hannah:
Something strange happened.

Lillian:
Something strange happened.

*Lillian lifts her sleeves, revealing a glittery sheen on her arms which Hannah examines.*

Lillian:  I woke up with these splotches. I hope I'm not contagious.

Hannah:  It appears to be an iridescent rash suffused with flecks of mica, like a good dusting by fairies. Does it itch?

Lillian:  No.

Hannah:  How far along is your pregnancy?

Lillian:  Nearly five months.

Hannah:  Have you had an amniocentesis?

Lillian:  Yes, everything's fine. I know they're twin girls; I'm naming them River and Rain.

Hannah:  Ah. You'll need to write down everything you've had to eat or drink in the past two weeks, and every place you've been.

Lillian:  I'm either here or my pool or the lab where I work.

Hannah:  Yes, I understand you're employed by the Atlantic Waters Institute.

Lillian: That's right; and please, call me Lillian. I'm working with a team of marine biologists. We're researching the major mass extinctions.

Hannah:  What about your husband? Has he had any illnesses?

Lillian:  I'm single; I was inseminated by an anonymous donor.

Hannah:  Ah. Well, Miss Lillian, I am afraid you are going to need blood tests, a biopsy, and an ultrasound. I will also need a list of the chemical contents of your laboratory and pool. *(Pause.)* Aside from the obvious, your blood pressure's low, your temperature's subnormal, and your pupils are dilated. Are you taking drugs?

Lillian:  No.

Hannah:  Anything you haven't told me?

Lillian:  I have trouble sleeping.

Hannah:  Anything else?

Lillian:  Well, I...I eat fish.

Hannah:  Ah. Which fish?

Lillian:  Oysters, clams, and...

Hannah:  Yes...?

Lillian:  Shrimp, shark, marlin, mackerel, and anything that swims!

Hannah:  My god, woman! That has to cease immediately! Surely you know fish can harbor parasites that cause toxoplasmosis; not to mention fetal deformities.

Lillian:  Yes, yes, but when River and Rain start kicking, I get cravings so intense; I can't seem to control myself. I know it sounds crazy, but they're the fish lovers. I always preferred poultry.

Hannah:  Do you have swollen glands or muscle aches?

Lillian:  No.

Hannah:  Any nausea?

Lillian:  No.

Hannah:  You realize you are at risk.

Lillian:  What can I do?

Hannah:  Nourish your babies 'bodies and minds. I'll prescribe vitamins and an antibiotic; then avoid the lab; eat sumptuous meals, but make certain the meat's well cooked! Now before I leave, there is something I must say: your breath, Miss Lillian, it is not pleasant.

> *As Hannah continues her testimony, Lillian fetches a hidden fishbowl, snatches a fish, and swallows.*

Her breath wasn't just foul, it was infectious; not just a nasty case of halitosis, but permeating my carpets, curtains, clothes and the rum colas I drank to calm my nerves. When I sobered up, I analyzed her skin sample: The epidermis was infused with mineral residue, ichthylepidin, and magnesium carbonate, in other words: fish scales! Two days later, Miss Lillian's rash was spreading, and since she refused to leave her house, I returned with my portable ultrasound.

> *Hannah wheels a portable sonogram towards Lillian who is lying supine.*

*(To Lillian.)* Now then, shall we see how River and Rain are progressing?

> *As Hannah places the probe on Lillian's stomach, lights reveal River and Rain wrapped head to toe in the transparent sheath of Lillian's amniotic sac. They appear to be swimming slowly, their limbs intertwined, intoning deep melodious, oceanic sounds.*

River and Rain: Uuuuuuuuloooooooolaaaaaaaaa...

Hannah: There they are.

Lillian: *(Sighs, relieved.)* Ohhhh, they're fine, perfectly normal. One of them seems to be waving.

Hannah:  Oh, dear...

Lillian:  What...?

Hannah:  Look closely: there appear to be membranes between the fingers; the toes as well!

Lillian:  Oh.

Hannah:  Now focus on their necks, beneath the ears...

Lillian:  You mean those small, narrow slits?

Hannah:  My God, they have gills! Membranes can be surgically removed, but gills...

Lillian:  But what if...?

Hannah:  What...?

Lillian: Well, if they're swimmers, they'll be useful. After all we humans possess our own inner fish. Through evolution our jaws and ear bones correspond exactly to the gill structures of fish, and it's not so noticeable, is it?

Hannah: Sorry, but I am not optimistic. Your test results indicate toxic levels of mercury and tetrodotoxin; you're also full of worms, mostly flukes and nematodes. Frankly, I amazed you're still breathing, much less functioning. Have you given any thought to terminating?

Lillian: No, absolutely not.

River and Rain: *(Squirming.)* Ohhhhhhhhhhhhhhh...

Lillian: After five attempts, I'm seeing this through. You're a mother; surely you understand.

Hannah:  Ah, but my children were not on their way to being a new species!

Lillian:  A species that will live in water as well as on land! They'll know the sea in a way we'll never know it.

Hannah:  Ah, you mean they won't need cumbersome scuba gear?

Lillian:  Not just that. Glaciers are melting which means oceans are rising, causing storms, floods; whole countries are shrinking! But no matter what happens, River and Rain will thrive. They'll thrive because they'll have two worlds to live in!

Hannah:  Good, because if they smell like you, no one will want to go near them!

River and Rain:  Whhhhhhhhhhhhhhhhhhhhhhaaahhh...

Lillian:  Can't you see?! River and Rain could expand our definition of humanity. We'll start thinking of ourselves as an evolving species; people will glimpse their future!

Hannah:  Or their past. If they're amphibious, they're regressive.

Lillian:  You're wrong; they'll make the whole of history swim faster!

Hannah:  Well, I won't be bobbing in their wake! Sorry, but they are malformed, undernourished, and likely to suffer developmental disorders, which means they'll need constant lifelong care. *(Pause.)* Oh, dear, now that they've turned, I see a projection from Rain's spine. Are my eyes playing tricks or does it seem to be extending? What is it? A cyst? A tumor...?

Lillian:  It's a fin! *(Delighted.)* A fin! A fin that reflects the ancestral bones that made our knees, our femurs, fibulas and tibias. Even the bones of our hands can be traced to the skeletons of fish! The primordial waters are still flowing! We have whole oceans inside us!

> *Hannah gapes, appalled, then turns to continue addressing the audience.*

Hannah:  I never thought they'd last to term, and confess I watched with morbid fascination. Four months passed; then clever Miss Lillian timed their births so we were trapped in her house where her inner ocean spewed forth River and Rain... straight into her pool!

> *Shimmering lights reveal a pool where River and Rain emit watery wails while breaking through their amniotic sac, then separate and land with a splash.*

Everything is tested when you deliver a child who's malformed: your prejudices and preconceptions, your emotional and physical stamina, your very notion of what constitutes human nature.

> *Hannah draws forth a large syringe.*

They have to be euthanized.

Lillian:  No! Out of the question!

Hannah:  No one has to know.

Lillian:  Stop it! Stop right now!

Hannah:  My God, woman, put them out of their misery!

Lillian:  I told you, no! Not now, not ever! All I want is for you to examine them.

Hannah:  They're too damn slippery! *(Pause.)* Well, we can both observe the obvious: they're blue, hairless, and warm blooded.

Lillian:  Like the higher marine mammals. I wonder if they're transgender... like blue headed wrasses who start out female then become male. Do you think they're sentient?

Hannah:  Let's hope not. Otherwise, they'll realize the age of mammals is in full swing, and they're not invited to the party. They will hate you!

> *Suddenly River and Rain sing a haunting melody.*

River and Rain: Whhaaa, la, la, loo, loo, loo...

Hannah: My God!

Lillian:  Incredible! They both sound so lovely...

Hannah:  Like bottom feeding divas! So what now? They're going to be hungry? Will you be feeding them fish bait?

Lillian:  Minced vegetables, minnows, and sea water. As soon as they learn to speak, stand upright, and are properly socialized, I'll present them to the world!

Hannah:  You'll what!?

Lillian:  There'll be a huge demand for their genes.

Hannah:  Are you saying you actually planned this?!

Lillian:  I've been working on the genomes for several piscine species. All I did was isolate the appropriate nucleotides and inject them into their embryos.

Hannah:  My God, woman! What you've done is reckless and reprehensible!

Lillian:  In a few years there'll be an even greater gender imbalance. Due to prenatal sex selection in China and India, there's already one hundred and twenty males born for every hundred females. Too many males means unstable countries with unstable armies dropping bombs which means more pollution, more warming, more flooding, so where will all the peace lovers of the world escape? To the lakes, rivers, and oceans! Of course we can't expose them until they've matured.

Hannah:  Ah! Then you'll expose them to ridicule, condemnation, and a media frenzy! Frankly, I think you've cracked your coconut!

Lillian:  Have I? You have to admit we humans have trashed the planet, and since we lack the will to modify our behavior, I've modified the species instead.  We may perish with the rest of the predators, but River and Rain will carry our genes. They'll be swimming in their aquatic Eden, leading us out of darkness and back to the sea!

*Pause as River and Rain cease singing and Hannah steps forward to speak in the present, followed by Lillian.*

Hannah:  That was twelve years ago, and though I agreed to remain the twins 'personal physician, I'm dead set against reproductive gene therapy of any kind! The media gossips call Doctor Sherborn a female Frankenstein, only instead of stitching cadavers, she incubated her creatures in her womb. After the immediate excitement died down, the only place that welcomed us was this carnival sideshow where the twins are known as The Tsunami Sisters; an appropriate name since they caused great waves of discourse and derision!

*Now Lillian approaches to speak to the audience.*

Lillian:  Now it's my turn: I'm here with the understanding that there were no enforceable laws in effect when I began my gestation, followed by years of nurturing my children who are not "creatures" but an extraordinary new species. So now ladies and gentlemen: may I present the world's first homo-piscines: River and Rain!

*River and Rain enter dancing, showing off their glittery, blue bodies, twirling their hands.*

Being part male, but mostly female, River and Rain produce both ova and sperm, spawning hundreds of eggs. Their eggs have hatched, been dispersed, and are swimming in the Caribbean Sea, then west in the Gulf of Mexico, the Pacific Ocean, then east in the Atlantic, New York Harbor and the Hudson River. They're intelligent, creative, and comprehend their unique nature. Before we leave, they want to sing for you.

> *River and Rain sing with warbling watery voices.*

RIVER and RAIN:

Somewhere in the water
Are my daughters swimming free;
Somewhere in the water
You can hear their melody.
They've gone to find a home among the fishes;
They've gone to find their lovers in the sea,
Oh, oh, oh, oh, oh,
In the sea,
Oh, oh, oh, oh, oh, oh,
In the sea...

> *Lights fade to black.*

**End of Play.**